STORIES *of the* SPIRIT *of* JUSTICE

STORIES *of the* SPIRIT *of* JUSTICE

JEMAR TISBY

ZONDERkidz

ZONDERKIDZ

Stories of the Spirit of Justice

Copyright © 2025 Jemar Tisby

Illustrations © Jemar Tisby

Published by Zonderkidz, 3950 Sparks Drive, Suite 101, Grand Rapids, MI 49546. Zonderkidz is a registered trademark of The Zondervan Corporation, L.L.C., a wholly owned subsidiary of HarperCollins Christian Publishing, Inc.

Requests for information should be addressed to customercare@harpercollins.com.

ISBN 978-0-310-14559-2 (hardcover)
ISBN 978-0-310-14562-2 (audio)
ISBN 978-0-310-14561-5 (ebook)

Library of Congress Control Number: 2024946280

Scripture quotations are taken from The Holy Bible, New International Version®, NIV®. Copyright © 1973, 1978, 1984, 2011 by Biblica, Inc.® Used by permission of Zondervan. All rights reserved worldwide. www.Zondervan.com. The "NIV" and "New International Version" are trademarks registered in the United States Patent and Trademark Office by Biblica, Inc.®

Zondervan titles may be purchased in bulk for educational, business, fundraising, or sales promotional use. For information, please email SpecialMarkets@Zondervan.com.

Cover Design: Kathy Mitchell/Kathy Mitchell Design
Interior and Cover Illustrations: Amanda Quartey
Interior Design: Kristen Sasamoto

Printed in the United States of America

24 25 26 27 28 LBC 5 4 3 2 1

CONTENTS

CONTENTS

The **ABOLITIONIST** MOVEMENT

The **CIVIL WAR** *and* RECONSTRUCTION

The **JIM CROW** ERA

The **CIVIL RIGHTS** ERA

The LATE TWENTIETH CENTURY

The EARLY TWENTY-FIRST CENTURY

AUTHOR'S NOTE

When I was in school, I don't think History or Social Studies were my favorite subjects. What I do remember is that I liked stories. I loved fantasy novels and adventure books. But I also liked hearing true stories from history, as long as the book I was reading or the teacher explaining them made it interesting. That's what I hope this book is for you—a bunch of interesting stories about real people and true history.

I'm a historian. My job is to learn about the past and then tell stories about it. Before I went back to school for a degree in history, I was a middle school teacher and, later, a principal. I know what it's like to feel like you don't have enough time to teach what the students need to learn—there's math, science, and gym classes, lunch periods, field trips, presentations, and so much you have to do in a school day. So this book is one way to share the stories your teachers didn't have the time to get to in class. Always remember, you can be in charge of your own education. You don't have to wait for permission to learn more. Follow your curiosity. Chase answers to your questions and see where they lead.

Reading *Stories of the Spirit of Justice* is the perfect way to follow your curiosity. Read this book in any order you want. You can skip around and go to the people who seem most interesting to you. Read as much or as little at one time as you like—one story, two or three, a whole section. It's up to you. One tip: try to read at the same time every day so you can get through the whole book. Whether it's in the morning, at lunchtime, right after school, or around bedtime, make reading a habit and you'll be surprised at how many books you get through.

A few of the folks in the book will probably stand out to you, and you'll want to find out more. That's exactly what I hope will happen. These stories are short; they are meant to just get you started. But you can go deeper after that. Do your own research at the library or on the internet to find out more. The more you learn about the past, the more you'll want to keep learning about it.

If you're looking for another book to read after this one, I also wrote *How to Fight Racism Young Readers Edition: A Guide to Standing for Racial Justice*. It gives you practical steps for how kids can resist racism. It's also full of other stories from history, so you'll learn about even more people from the past.

I hope these stories are interesting to you. But I also hope for more. I want you to read these stories and see that ordinary people, people just like you and me, can do the important work of fighting racism and making the world better for all people. The figures in this book can be your cheerleaders, clapping for you and shouting encouragement from the past to help you work for good in the present. We still face a lot of problems today, and you can be part of the solution.

I want to encourage you right now. You're taking a big step by reading this book. Not many kids would pick up a book about history and race. But you already see these subjects are important and you are going above and beyond to grow your knowledge. That's special. You are precisely the kind of person who can end up in a history book for the important, hope-filled work you will do in life. I don't know the future, but I can say with confidence that tomorrow can be better than today because the spirit of justice lives in people like you. Thanks for reading.

INTRODUCTION

She looked like a queen. Her short black hair was scattered with gray, and she wore a red and black scarf draped across her shoulders like a regal robe. She held herself with such dignity and elegance that the wheelchair she sat on seemed like a throne. Her name was Myrlie Evers-Williams.

On this day—December 9, 2017—Evers-Williams was holding court with more than a dozen journalists from across the nation. The occasion was the grand opening of the Mississippi Civil Rights Museum in Jackson, the first state-sponsored museum in the country dedicated to the history of Black civil rights, and I had the honor of being in the room with Myrlie Evers-Williams as she spoke.

What should have been a happy event was clouded with controversy. At the time, Donald J. Trump was president. He had been invited to attend by Mississippi's governor, Phil Bryant, but many people did not like the idea of President Trump appearing at the grand opening. He had often been accused of speaking and acting in racist ways. Some well-known guests refused to attend, including Representative Bennie Thompson—who served the district where the museum is located—and Representative John Lewis—who had marched with Martin Luther King Jr. and headed the Student Nonviolent Coordinating Committee (SNCC). But Myrlie Evers-Williams still came.

Most people know Myrlie Evers-Williams as the widow of Medgar Evers. He had been the field secretary for the National Association for the Advancement of Colored People (NAACP) in Mississippi, and was shot and killed by a white man in front of their home in Jackson on

June 12, 1963. He gave his life for his work promoting voting rights and Black civil rights.

Medgar Evers was born in Decatur, Mississippi, in 1925 and started working for the NAACP in 1954. Mississippi was known as the most racist state in the US. But Evers bravely helped organize people to push for racial justice. After the brutal lynching of Emmett Till, a fourteen-year-old from Chicago who had been accused of whistling at a white woman, Evers dressed up like a farmworker to gather eyewitness accounts from Black sharecroppers of what had happened. He helped another man named James Meredith become the first Black person to attend the University of Mississippi. He met Myrlie in college, and together they helped establish the NAACP in Mississippi.

After Medgar's murder, Myrlie Evers-Williams continued the civil rights work that she'd begun with her husband. As a widow and a single mom, she moved her family to California and ran for Congress there twice. In the 1990s, she returned to the NAACP and became chair of the board, helping steer the organization back to health. President Barack Obama invited her to give the invocation, or opening prayer, at his second inauguration ceremony in 2013—she was the first woman and the first person who wasn't a pastor or a priest to have this honor.

Now she was back in her home state of Mississippi at the opening of a museum that was not only sharing history, it was sharing the history of her *family*—her husband's assassination, the news coverage afterward, the court cases attempting to convict his killer, the pain her family faced after it was completely changed with the pull of a trigger. Even at eighty-four years old, and after all she had seen in her life, Evers-Williams still sounded hopeful. "Going through the museums, I wept because I felt the blows, I felt the bullets, I felt the tears, I felt the cries. But I also sensed the hope that dwelt in all those people," she said. I could hardly believe her optimism, especially because the museum exhibited the gun that had been used to kill her husband and shatter her life more than fifty years ago.

After her speech that was televised to thousands, Myrlie took time to answer questions from the press in a smaller gathering. Someone asked her how she thought the present-day state of race relations compared to what she saw in the civil rights movement of the 1950s and 1960s. I'm glad I was there, and I'm glad I was recording her words, because they helped inspire this book.

"I see something today that I had hoped I would never see again. That is prejudice, hatred, negativism that comes from the highest points across America," she told us. Then, with the honesty that comes with old age, she said, "And I found myself asking Medgar in the conversations that I have with him, 'Is this really what's happening again in this country?' And asking for guidance because—I don't mind admitting this to the press—I'm a little weary at this point."

Of course she was weary. She had been in the struggle for racial justice longer than many of us had been alive. Her husband's life was stolen just because he wanted Black people to have equal rights. She had dedicated giant amounts of time and energy to making the world a better place, and now it seemed like everything was going backward. But she saw it differently.

"[I]t's something about the spirit of justice that raises up like a war horse. That horse that stands with its back sunk in and hears that bell—I like to say the 'bell of freedom.' And all of a sudden, it becomes straight, and the back becomes stiff. And you become determined all over again."

In the years since that day, I have often come back to a phrase Myrlie Evers-Williams used: the spirit of justice. In my work as a historian, I have noticed that in every age of US history, people have risen up to resist racism. They face seemingly impossible obstacles and experience setback after setback, but they still keep going. In the Bible, when Jesus calmed a raging storm just by telling it to stop, his followers asked in amazement, "What kind of man is this?" In a similar way, when we see people like Myrlie Evers-Williams and countless others throughout history calmly face the storms of hatred and prejudice, we ask, "What kind of people are these?" The answer is these are the people who have the spirit of justice—the heartbeat of people who hunger and thirst for righteousness. The spirit of people who will not give up. The strength of those who never stop never stopping.

The spirit of justice is the inner force that moves us to demand dignity and respect for ourselves and others. It is the cry of our souls for the world to be a fair and kind place. It is the power that inspires people to speak up when others remain silent. To move when others stand still. To put themselves on the line when others choose to remain comfortable.

The spirit of justice belongs to all of us, and you have access to it right now. Reading this book will help you become a leader on the journey toward racial justice. We study history to recognize how the spirit of justice was at work in the past so we can continue the struggle against racism in the present. Fighting racism is not for the weak. But you are stronger than you realize because you have the spirit of justice.

The
COLONIAL ERA
1492–1765

In elementary school, I learned this rhyme: "In 1492, Columbus sailed the ocean blue." I don't know if they still teach that, but I think the next year—1493—is more important. That is when Pope Alexander VI, the head of the Roman Catholic Church, wrote an official letter that explained the "doctrine of discovery." As Mark Charles and Soong-Chan Rah explained in their book *Unsettling Truths*, the pope told Europeans it was alright with God if they took over the lands where non-Christian people lived. "The pope offered a spiritual validation for European conquest."

The voyages of people like Christopher Columbus and others in the 1400s and 1500s were not just about adventure or exploration—they were about money. Europeans knew that lands far from Europe had rich natural resources and products that would be worth a lot of money. The plan was to trade with the people in places such as North America and make a profit. But if trading didn't work or wasn't profitable enough, they could conquer the people and steal their resources. That was a brutal process, and it went against the spirit of Jesus's teachings—at least it was seen that way until the pope wrote his letter.

His letter allowed people to believe that God, the creator of the universe, blessed European plans to build colonies and take away resources, even if it meant using violence. This is why many people treated Native Americans and Africans so badly. They thought that God made Europeans superior to darker-skinned people of other nations and that conquering these lands was a way to spread the Christian religion. In their minds, if they got rich in the process, then that was just God's blessing.

The colonial era was a time when European nations such as Spain, Portugal, England, France, and others set up colonies in North America. It is a time when racism and slavery were just being formed and when Africans, stolen from their homelands, first encountered America.

African American history does not start with slavery in North America—it starts with Africans in Africa. Today, the continent of Africa is made up of fifty-four different countries, fifteen hundred different languages or dialects, more than three thousand different tribes, and so much land you can fit three United States inside the continent. So there is no "one" Africa. It is a massive land that contains all kinds of people.

Before the start of slavery in the United States, people in Africa had rich and interesting lives. They built incredible cities, created beautiful art, and made their own choices. One of the richest men in the history of the world was from Africa! His name was Mansa Musa, and he was the ruler of the empire of Mali. He had more gold than anyone had ever seen. He practiced the religion of Islam. In 1324, he journeyed across Africa to Mecca, an Islamic holy site, with a group of sixty thousand people. They had eighty camels and each of them carried three hundred pounds of gold. Gold is seen as valuable because there is not a lot of it and it is very hard to get. But when Mansa Musa went through Egypt, he spent so much gold there that, for a little while, it was not worth much because there was so much of it around.

Africans also had their own religions and gods long before they ever came into contact with European slave traders. Many had a belief in Orishas—supernatural entities that took many forms, including gods, ancestors who had died, or forces in the natural world. Africans also believed in religions such as Islam and Christianity. Europeans divided the world into Christian and non-Christian people. But they ignored the rich religion and spirituality that Africans already had.

You will often hear the year 1619 as the start of the African slave trade in North America. This is the year when a Dutch trading ship brought "20. And odd Negroes" to Point Comfort in Virginia. But these were not the first Africans brought across the Atlantic. For more than one hundred years, Europeans had been forcefully transporting Africans to places such as Haiti, Jamaica, and Brazil. But 1619 is still important because it marks a clear date when Africans had to start figuring out what it meant to be both African and American.

In those times, it was not clear what place Africans would have in the North American colonies. Everyone was still figuring it out. The Africans brought to Virginia were definitely not free. They were treated like property and traded for supplies the sailors who brought them needed. But slavery as we now understand it had not been created. These Africans may have been treated like "indentured servants."

An indentured servant was a laborer who was required to work for someone for a certain number of years. You became an indentured servant if you had a debt you could not pay or as punishment for a crime. Being an indentured servant was hard work. You had to do whatever the person in charge of you said, and you did not get paid. But it had an end date. You could work your way out of servitude. And usually you could legally get married, own property, and have other rights. In the colonial era, Africans worked for people according to those rules. Slavery—which lasted your entire life, depended on skin color, saw you as property and not as a person, and was inherited through your mother's status as free or enslaved—was still being formed.

In the stories of the people who lived during this era, we see the spirit of justice arise in Africans who were forced onto slave ships and brought to North America. They resisted their bondage from the very first days of contact with Europeans. They held on to their African beliefs while still learning to survive in a place that was an ocean away from the land of their birth.

While Europeans were building their colonies, Africans in America were building new identities. They struggled to hold on to their languages, cultures, and religions from Africa while also adapting to forced labor in a new and very strange land. They were *becoming* African American.

ANTHONY, ISABELLA, *and* WILLIAM
1625

Marching and protesting are not the only ways to fight injustice. Sometimes the most important acts of resistance are the simplest ones—like having a family. During the slave trade it was very difficult for African families to stay together. They faced separation on the continent of Africa when brothers, sisters, mothers, fathers, and other relatives were captured and sorted onto different slave ships. Slave traders separated families when they sold people in different parts of South America, the Caribbean islands, and North America. Even on the plantation, an enslaver could decide one day to break a family apart by selling members to different plantations. In these conditions, the Black family is a sort of everyday miracle.

Records show that among a group of twenty or so Africans who were traded to British colonists in Virginia in 1619 were a man named Anthony and a woman named Isabella. Religion is part of their story since their names were probably given or changed when they were baptized into the Catholic Church. A few years later in 1625, the government did an official count—a census—of the people who lived in the colony. The census noted that Anthony and Isabella were married, and they had a son.

The exact note read, "Antoney Negro: Isabell Negro: and William Theire Child Baptized." These nine words tell a much larger story. First, no one in the family has a last name listed. Europeans usually had their full names recorded because they were considered full persons by law. But Africans were considered property and lifelong laborers for Europeans. The census-takers likely did not record the last names of Anthony, Isabella, or William because Africans were not seen as important, so they may not have known their last names. Or the names may be missing because Africans were simply identified by the last name of their European enslaver. In this note they are simply called "Negro."

Another important piece of the story this note tells is that Anthony and Isabella had a child. This might not seem like a big deal. People around the world have children every day. But William may be the first child born to an African couple in British-settled North America. As a child born to Africans in America, William could be the first truly "African American" child. William's religion is important as well. The note says that he was "baptized." This means he was a Christian. Being a Christian in this time meant that William and his parents might one day gain their freedom.

European Christians in the colonial era had a tradition that said you should not enslave other Christians. Even though William and his parents were African, being Christians gave them the opportunity to pursue their freedom on the grounds that fellow Christians should not hold other Christians against their will. It was certainly better in those days to be considered Christian than a "heathen"—a person who did not worship God or worshiped other gods.

We cannot know for sure what motivated Anthony and Isabella to bring a child into the world. And we cannot know exactly how they felt about starting a family in a land far away from home and strange to them. But there is no reason to think they thought about their newborn child any differently than other families would. As they looked lovingly at their son, they would have wanted him to be healthy, treat others kindly, and grow up to be a happy human being in his work, family, and community. Even though they had been forced away from their homeland in Africa, they would have tried to make the best of the situation and raise their child with love and tenderness.

Having a family and raising children in a society that considers you "less than" and enslaves your people is an act of resistance. Growing a family requires thinking about the future and protecting a sense of hope that tomorrow can be better than today. And during slavery, it required faith that your children could find a way to thrive in a society that was against them in so many ways. Children represent the hope and humanity of all people, and for Black people they are a living example that the spirit of justice will be passed down from one generation to the next.

JOHN PUNCH

1605–Unknown

Do you like to invent new games and make up the rules? Or pretend to be someone or something else, like a knight, a queen, or a shark? When you play, you use your imagination. You understand that the things you pretend aren't real, they're make-believe. But what if you didn't know it was make-believe? What if you forgot that you were imagining and you thought the game was real? That's what happened with the invention of race.

Race is made up. A person's skin color has nothing to do with how hard they work, how creative they can be, or what opportunities they deserve. How light or dark our skin is depends on the amount of a chemical we have called melanin. There is also nothing in Christianity that says what a person looks like matters to God. In fact, the Bible says that we should not judge people based on outward appearances but based on the heart (1 Samuel 16:7). So how was race made up? How did we forget that it was imaginary and make it so meaningful?

Part of the answer to how race, this made-up category, became real has to do with how we made laws. To say that race is "made up" does not mean people did not notice differences before racism was created. They saw the differences in skin color. They knew they spoke different languages, dressed differently, and came from different parts of the world. And people still hated one another for being different. But in those days, opportunities and prejudices did not usually have to do with skin color. That came later, when people started making laws about racism. The laws people passed back in the 1600s helped create categories such as "Black" or "white." This is what happened in the case of John Punch.

John Punch was not a slave. He was an indentured servant of African descent. We only know a little about him—he was born around 1605 and he labored in Virginia for British man named Hugh Gwyn. We're not sure what kind of labor he did or when he died. Though we do know what life was like for an indentured servant.

Being an indentured servant was very similar to being enslaved. These women and men worked without pay. They had to face a lack of food, near nakedness, whippings, and harsh working conditions. Usually, someone became an indentured servant as punishment for a crime or to pay off a debt. But indentured servitude was not for a lifetime. Eventually an indentured servant finished their sentence and was released.

Even though indentured servitude was not slavery, it was clearly not pleasant at all. It was so bad for John Punch that he and two other indentured servants—James Gregory and Victor—ran away from their "master" in 1640. After just a few days, the authorities caught up with the fugitives and put them on trial.

The court ruled that the three men were guilty of running away from their labor as indentured servants. As a punishment, James Gregory and Victor both received whippings and had four more years of labor added on to their indentured servitude. The consequence for John Punch, however, was different. In addition to a whipping, the court decided that Punch would have to "serve his said master or his assigns for the time of his natural life here or elsewhere." That meant that John Punch would have to labor for a lifetime without pay. In other words, he had gone from being an indentured servant who could one day obtain his freedom to a slave for life.

Why did John Punch get such a harsh verdict from the court? He had run away, but so had the other two indentured servants. So why didn't they all get the same sentence? In a word—race. James Gregory was Scottish and Victor was Dutch. They were of European descent and considered white. John Punch had African ancestry and was labeled Black. The only difference between the men was their skin color, and the person with darker skin—the Black person—got a lifetime sentence. This court case likely makes John Punch the first person *legally* considered Black in the United States.

We do not know how John Punch reacted to the verdict. Maybe he became sad and gave up trying to resist his bondage. Maybe he was determined to make another escape attempt. Maybe he decided to make the best of his circumstances. What we do know for sure is that people considered Black had a lower status than people considered white when it came to the law. Court cases like John Punch's were another step toward making the make-believe idea of race into a real category with real consequences in the real world. Yet despite this injustice, the spirit of justice would live on in the hearts of those who refused to accept a human-made, subordinate status based purely on the color of their skin.

OLAUDAH EQUIANO,
or GUSTAVUS VASSA
1745–1797

Imaging having two names: one name that you were given at birth by your parents and another name given by someone who claimed to buy you and own you. It would be confusing. You would struggle to understand your identity because you had two names that were given in very different circumstances. That is precisely the dilemma Olaudah Equiano faced.

In 1745, an African boy of the Igbo tribe (present-day Nigeria) was born. His name was Olaudah Equiano. When he was just eleven years old, he was kidnapped by white slave traders and sold into slavery. Slaveholders often gave enslaved Africans new names. One reason was that they came from Europe or North America, and they didn't feel like learning to correctly pronounce African names. Another reason was that a new name created distance between an enslaved African and their home culture and language. Renaming someone was like giving them a new identity. One of Equiano's slaveholders named him Gustavus Vassa. But Equiano never forgot his birth name or his African Igbo identity.

That's probably why Equiano's autobiography—the story of his life—had such a long title. It was called *The Interesting Narrative of the Life of Olaudah Equiano, or Gustavus Vassa, the African.* Equiano (or Vassa) uses both his names in the title because he writes about the two lives he had under those two names. First, he tells readers about his life in Africa, and then he lets them know about his life under slavery in both North America and Britain.

Although Equiano was very young when he was stolen from his homeland, he still had memories of growing up in Africa. He remembered his home as a "charming fruitful vale." Equiano described weddings in his tribe. Instead of a woman getting a wedding ring at the marriage ceremony, "they tie[d] round her waist a cotton string the thickness of a goose-quill, which none but married women are permitted to wear." Equiano also wrote about his people's love for music and dancing. "We are almost a nation of dancers, musicians, and poets."

Equiano and his sister were kidnapped together but the slavers soon separated them. "It was in vain that we besought them not to part us," he wrote. "She was torn from me, and immediately carried away . . . I cried and grieved continually; and for several days, I did not eat anything but what they forced into my mouth." After several months, the traders finally took Equiano aboard a slave ship. Upon seeing so many light-skinned Europeans, hearing their strange language, and gazing on the vastness of the ocean for the first time, Equiano fainted.

The slave ship took Equiano from Africa to a group of islands in the Caribbean Sea called the West Indies, and after that an enslaver in Virginia purchased him. We now call the journey kidnapped Africans were forced to take the "Middle Passage," which traveled from the west coast of Africa to places in North America, Central America, and the Caribbean. Equiano and hundreds of other enslaved Africans were dragged below deck. He wrote, "The closeness of the place, and the heat of the climate, added to the number in the ship, which was so crowded that each had scarcely the room to turn himself, almost suffocated us." There were no bathrooms. Whenever someone had to go, they used a massive tub "into which the children often fell and were almost suffocated." During the slave trade, the Middle Passage lasted several weeks and, in some cases, several months. During this horrible journey, many Africans died and their bodies were simply thrown overboard.

That was only the beginning of the terror for enslaved Africans. After arriving on the other side of the Atlantic Ocean, slave traders sold Africans to white people. The Africans never knew who would purchase them or where they would end up. Equiano's enslaver was a sailor, who put the young boy to work on a ship sailing for England. One day, after thirteen weeks of travel, Equiano came up from below deck and saw a cold, white powder covering every surface. The climate in Equiano's home was hot, so he had never seen or heard of snow. Equiano asked a white sailor what it was and where it came from: "He told me a great man in the heavens, called God." Eventually, Equiano learned more about Christianity and came to believe in Jesus.

Unfortunately, many of the slaveholders who forced Equiano to work for them and the other Europeans he saw in his many travels called themselves Christians but did not act anything like followers of Jesus. When Equiano was around twelve years old, he was put up for sale at a slave auction for the first time. The European slave traders rushed into a courtyard and snatched up the human beings they wanted to buy. They paid no attention to family relationships and separated brothers, sisters, and cousins. Years later Equiano wrote, "O, ye nominal Christians! might not an African ask you, learned you this from your God, who says unto you, Do unto all men as you would men should do unto you?" He was asking how people who claim to be Christians can treat people so differently from how they would like to be treated. Equiano used his writing to point out the failings of Christians who claimed to love God and to love their neighbors but also chose to enslave people.

Even though slave-holding European Christians set a bad example, Equiano often talked positively about his Christian faith. It is what carried him through the difficulties of being ripped from his homeland and forced into slavery. It is what gave him the strength and courage to make the best of a life he did not choose for himself. He "looked up with prayers anxiously to God" for his liberty. To Equiano, "The word of

God was sweet to my taste, yea sweeter than honey and the honeycomb. Christ was revealed to my soul as the chiefest among ten thousand." Nothing in life was as important to Equiano as Jesus.

Equiano was sold to different slaveholders throughout his life and worked mostly on British trading ships. Eventually, one of Equiano's slaveholders allowed him to do his own business on the side, trading common goods and foods for a profit. It took him several years, but Equiano saved enough money to buy his own freedom in 1766. He continued sailing on and off during his career as a free man, and eventually settled in England.

We know about Olaudah Equiano's life today because of his autobiography—in this case, it is seen a special type of writing about life under enslavement called a "slave narrative." Equiano's slave narrative was published in 1789 and became an international sensation that was read in many countries. It helped bring attention to the evil of slavery and convinced people to resist it. For the rest of his life, until his death in 1797, Equiano shared his story of kidnapping, enslavement, freedom, and faith in God to call for the abolition of slavery and the good of his African brothers and sisters.

The
REVOLUTIONARY ERA
1765–1783

There is a saying among authors—writing is revising. When you write, the first draft is only a start. Your words get better when you read your work again and again to get each sentence and paragraph just right. This is simply how the writing process works in most cases. But sometimes you can cut out the wrong words when you are revising. This is what happened with the Declaration of Independence.

In 1776, the British colonists in North America had enough. They were tired of the British leader, King George III, who was making rules about the colonies while he was all the way across the Atlantic. They especially hated all the taxes the king was demanding they pay. They were finally ready to officially break up with Britain, so they wrote a statement to make it official. The first version of the Declaration of Independence included an important paragraph against slavery. Thomas Jefferson, who wrote most of the document, said:

> [King George III] has waged cruel war against human nature itself, violating its most sacred rights of life and liberty in the persons of a distant people who never offended him, captivating and carrying them into slavery in another hemisphere, or to incur miserable death in their transportation thither.

That's old-time language saying that one problem the colonists had with King George was his support of the African slave trade. They said it went against the "sacred rights of life and liberty" of human beings. During the transatlantic trip on slave ships, the result for Africans was often "miserable death."

But Thomas Jefferson, the author of this paragraph, enslaved hundreds of Africans during his lifetime. And slavery was legal and becoming more common in the colonies. A hypocrite is a person who says one thing and does another. In this case Jefferson and the colonists writing the Declaration of Independence were being hypocrites by saying that King George was wrong for encouraging the slave trade while the colonists engaged in slavery themselves.

It did not matter in the end, though. In the process of revising the Declaration of Independence, officials from southern states— where slavery was more widespread—demanded that the paragraph be removed, or they would not agree to sign the document. But imagine if the writers had kept it in. That single paragraph might have made race-based chattel slavery much harder to practice in the new United States of America. It would have at least raised serious questions about why people in the US could practice slavery when they called out King George and Britain for it. Maybe it would have even prevented the Civil War.

Although we'll never know what *could* have happened, we know what actually *did* happen. Slavery remained the law of the United States for decades to come. But that does not mean everyone was happy about it. Black people used the same arguments the colonists used against Britain to argue against slavery.

The most well-known words of the Declaration of Independence read, "We hold these truths to be self-evident, that all men are created equal, that they are endowed by their Creator with certain unalienable Rights, that among these are Life, Liberty and the pursuit of Happiness." Black people asked the European colonists, "Who was included in the words 'all men'?" And they protested that Black people, just like Europeans, had the right to life, liberty, and the pursuit of happiness. Black people argued that slavery had no place in a nation that said it valued freedom.

The colonists insisted on their own right to freedom from Britain's rule. They even declared that if Britain continued taxing the colonies, it would be like slavery. The colonists insisted on their liberty and fought the Revolutionary War to gain their independence. They demanded their rights, but in practice, the liberty they wanted only applied to a very small group of people—rich white men who owned property. Some colonists thought that only very wealthy men should rule the country. Their vision of freedom did not include women, the poor, or Native Americans. It certainly did not include enslaved Africans. European colonists used the language of liberty only for themselves, and even passed laws to further enslave Black people.

The Revolutionary era was a time in US history when the spirit of justice inspired Black people and their friends to use the principles of the Declaration of Independence and the war against Britain to make a case for emancipation. The Revolutionary era was also a time when some white Christians offered early arguments opposing slavery and built the foundation for the later era calling for the abolition of slavery in the early 1800s.

MUM BETT/
ELIZABETH FREEMAN

1744–1829

Many people think the backbreaking, sweaty work of picking cotton or har-
vesting crops was harder than working inside a white person's home.
But American slavery took place in the age before dishwashers and vac-
uum cleaners—which meant all the chores had to be done by hand.
The day often started before the sun came up because enslaved people
in the home had to get the day's work started before their white slaveholders woke up. They cooked, cleaned, washed, cared for the children,
and much more. In addition, these enslaved people did not have any
privacy. To make the situation even worse, they were always under the
watchful eye of their enslavers, who would yell at or beat an enslaved
person for tiniest mistake.

But there were some advantages of working inside a white person's
home. Sometimes you got to overhear important conversations. That's
what happened to Mum Bett/Elizabeth Freeman. She was born into
slavery in the 1740s and sent to labor for the Ashley family of Sheffield,
Massachusetts, likely when she was a teenager. She was called Bett,
but eventually received the nickname Mum Bett, and it stuck with her
for many years. She got married and had a daughter, but her husband

died fighting in the American Revolution when the American colonists fought for their independence from Britain.

Mum Bett's life was hard, especially because Mrs. Ashely, the woman of the home, treated her and her daughter, Betsy, so harshly. Once, Mrs. Ashley got so angry that she tried to hit another household slave (possibly Bett's sister or daughter) with a heated shovel. Mum Bett stepped in front of the household slave, and the shovel hit her instead. It made an ugly wound on her arm. Mum Bett left the wound uncovered to show everyone the kind of abuse she had to endure.

One day, after the Revolutionary War was over and the United States was establishing itself as an independent country, Mum Bett was in the house and overheard Mr. Ashley and his friends talking about the Bill of Rights and the brand-new Massachusetts Constitution. It said, "All men are born free and equal, and have certain natural, essential, and unalienable rights; among which may be reckoned the right of enjoying and defending their lives and liberties . . ."

When she heard this statement about rights and liberty, Mum Bett immediately thought of her own enslavement and her desire to be free. She found a white lawyer who was against slavery named Theodore Sedgwick and asked him for help. Together with another enslaved man named Brom, they sued for Mum Betts's freedom in a case called Brom and Bett v. Ashley. They argued their case based on Massachusetts' own government documents. A jury of community members had to listen to the case and decide Mum Bett's fate. Juries can argue and debate for days or even weeks before coming to a decision, if they end up agreeing at all. In Bett's case, the jury took only one day, and on August 22, 1781, they ruled in her favor. She became the first Black woman to sue and gain her freedom under the new state constitution. Her court case became the legal standard that eventually led to the end of slavery in Massachusetts in 1783.

Once she was free, Mum Bett took the name Elizabeth Freeman. Her last name spoke to her new status as a free person, and many other Black people would take the name Freeman for the same reason. She also went to work for Mr. Sedgwick, but this time she was a paid worker. She eventually saved up enough money to buy a house for her and her family, and became known throughout the area as a nurse, midwife, and healer.

After her trial, Elizabeth Freeman said, "Any time while I was a slave, if one minute's freedom had been offered to me, and I had been told I must die at the end of that minute, I would have taken it—just to stand one minute on God's [earth] a free woman—I would." Freedom was so precious that she would have given anything to get it for herself, her family, and all Black people. She displayed the spirit of justice by challenging slavery according to the Constitution and the nation's founding principles—and she won.

PHILLIS WHEATLEY
1753?–1784

Phillis Wheatley was born in the 1750s in West Africa. Only Phillis was not her real name, of course. While she was still a young girl, she was kidnapped like so many others and sold into slavery. The slave traders put her on a ship named the *Phillis*. When it arrived in Boston Harbor, a rich merchant and tailor named John Wheatley bought the girl to serve his daughter. He named her "Phillis" after the ship that brought her and "Wheatley" so she had his last name as a sign of ownership.

Most enslaved people were not allowed to learn how to read or write. In slaveholders' minds, reading books was a waste of time for enslaved people who had other work to do. Reading also gave enslaved people dangerous ideas about freedom and equality.

But Phillis Wheatley had the rare opportunity to learn how to read and write. This kind of education happened sometimes because enslaved people and their white enslavers worked together so closely. On rare occasions, someone in the house would think it was important for an enslaved person to learn some basic reading and writing skills. But this was never a popular idea and was not an opportunity most enslaved people could expect. Wheatley was able to read so much that she started writing her own words, especially poetry. At first, her white slaveholders helped her get published in local newspapers.

At some point in her young life, Phillis became a Christian. Her faith in Christ showed up in her art, and she did not separate her creative passion from her devotion to Jesus. Her poetry showed how hard it was for Africans in early America to make sense of Christianity. Even though they heard about the God of love, they learned religion from people who held them as slaves and who believed that Black people were inferior to white people. They learned about a Jesus who seemed to value you more if you dressed, spoke, and acted more like Europeans than Africans, and a God who cared deeply for their eternal salvation but seemingly not for their physical liberation.

Wheatley put her faith and her skill with words in service to her fellow enslaved Africans, arguing for their freedom. In October of 1772, she wrote a poem called "To the Right Honourable William, Earl of Dartmouth." Wheatley used this opportunity to flatter the earl, and to make an even more important point—that he should use his new power and position to free enslaved people.

> No longer shall thou dread the iron chain,
> Which wanton Tyranny with lawless hand
> Had made, and with it meant t'enslave the land.

But even as a teenager, her poetry was so good that many people doubted a Black woman could have written it. In 1772, a group of eighteen white men assembled at the Wheatley house. These men included Thomas Hutchinson, who was the governor of Massachusetts, and John Hancock, who would later be one of the men who signed the original Declaration of Independence. After they questioned her, they believed she had written the poems and wrote a signed letter of support. But even this was not enough. When Wheatley penned her first volume of poetry, called *Poems on Various Subjects, Religious and Moral*, no one in North America would publish it. Through the help of some white allies in England, she finally got it published there in 1773. When the work was published in North America in 1774, Phillis Wheatley became the first enslaved Black woman to publish a book of poetry in the future United States. Within a year of publishing her book, Wheatley's slaveholder freed her. She was just twenty-five years old.

Wheatley stands as an early voice in a long line of Black artists who used their creativity to imagine new worlds, argue for greater rights, and elevate humanity in a way that only true beauty can do. Though she was an enslaved Black person, her exceptional skills afforded her the opportunity to publish her work and achieve notoriety. Yet what many white people refused to see was the countless other Black people who had exceptional talents as well. These people simply lacked the same education and opportunity.

Even with Wheatley's brilliant mind, she was never able to secure a stable existence for herself or her family. Her poetic genius was more of a novelty than a reason for people to reevaluate their treatment of Black people or even to support Wheatley herself.

Wheatley got married but lived on the brink of poverty. Her first two children died at a very young age. Her husband died. Then she died in 1784 at the age of thirty-one, and her third son, an infant, died shortly after. Wheatley's hardships throughout life, especially after her emancipation, suggests that even white people who noticed her brilliance and appreciated her poetry did not see Africans in America needed ongoing economic or artistic support in order to survive. Did they truly support Black people or just use them for their art and skills?

Even after her death, the spirit of justice shines forth in her poetry. We see it in her strong desire for freedom, her use of the arts to overturn ideas of Black inferiority, and in her unshakeable faith in a God who remains active in human affairs.

PRINCE HALL
1735 or 1738–1807

When Prince Hall, a Black leader in the Revolutionary era, wrote about the "mild religion of Jesus," he meant the gentle, peaceful, loving way that Jesus treated people. Hall used the mild religion of Jesus as a reason to release enslaved people and honor that full humanity as Christ would.

We don't know a lot about Prince Hall's origin story. He was born in either 1735 or 1738, likely in New England, but perhaps in Barbados. Historians know he was enslaved at an early age by William Hall, a leather-worker in Boston who trained young Prince in the trade. Eventually, Prince was freed and became one of the most prominent Black men in late-1700s Massachusetts. He started a school for Black children in his own home, called for the release of free Black people who had been captured and forced into slavery, and was one of the early supporters of Black people going back to Africa to find a better life in their homeland.

Hall is best known for forming the first Black freemason lodge in North America. The freemasons are a members-only men's club that encourages friendships and community service. They are famous for being very secretive, and members do not talk to outsiders about their activities. At the time, all the freemason clubs in North America were for white men only. When Prince Hall helped start the first freemason club for Black men in 1775, it became a strong advocate for the abolition of slavery. The first chapter was located in Boston and called the African Grand Lodge #1. The Prince Hall Freemasons, as they are called, are the "oldest recognized and continuously active organization founded by African Americans." Hall was also a Christian who used Jesus's teachings to make the case for abolishing slavery.

In 1777, Hall helped write a famous letter to the Massachusetts General Assembly asking for emancipation. In it he writes that "a great number of Blackes" in a "free & Christian country" understand that "they have in common with all other men a natural and unalienable right to freedom." In this section of the petition, Hall echoes the words of the Declaration of Independence, which said, "We hold these truths to be self-evident, that all men are created equal, that they are endowed by their Creator with certain unalienable Rights, that among these are Life, Liberty and the pursuit of Happiness." But he roots his call for freedom in the equality of all humankind as given by the Creator, God, whom he calls the "Great Parent of the [Universe]." Hall goes on to argue that God has "bestowed equalley" freedom on all people. He appeals to white people as fellow Christians and writes, "A people professing the mild religion of Jesus . . . need not be informed that a life of slavery . . . is far worse than non-existence." As Hall understood it, Jesus would not want people to be enslaved, and anyone who called themselves a follower of Jesus should support the abolition of slavery. The white leaders of the government ignored Hall's petition at the time, but it was part of other protest efforts that would finally lead to the abolition of slavery in the state in 1783.

Hall used his prominence to advocate for individuals as well as the abolition of slavery. One important case he spoke into was that of a woman named Belinda Royall (also known as Belinda Sutton), who had been kidnapped from Africa and enslaved in Massachusetts for fifty years. Her slaveholder, a man who remained loyal to Britain during the Revolutionary War, fled his lands after the American patriots won. He left Belinda, whose face was "marked with the furrows of time" and was now elderly and caring for a sick daughter, with nothing. But she went to court and demanded a yearly retirement paycheck of fifteen pounds and twelve shillings.

Prince Hall wrote the petition to the Massachusetts General Court and argued that Belinda should receive her pay. She had worked for decades as a slave and had never been paid, but her slaveholder got rich partly through her labor. Hall wrote in his letter to the court that all enslaved people deserved "that freedom which the Almighty Father intended for all the human Race." In the end, Belinda won her case and secured financial support for her and her daughter. Prince Hall had won one of the earliest and only cases of reparations for a formerly enslaved person. (*Reparation* means "repair.") Although nothing could make up for the years of slavery Belinda had to endure, at least the courts recognized her right to some money for her work.

Prince Hall used his writing, the Black freemasons, and his faith to advance the cause of Black people in the early United States. Along with many other Black Christians, Hall saw in his religion the foundation to demand freedom based on a belief that God had created all people as equals and with the universal right to make choices for themselves. Hall also drew on ideas of liberty that were part of the Revolutionary War to challenge the new nation to extend the freedoms they had won from the British to Black Americans and advance the spirit of justice.

JEAN BAPTISTE POINT DU SABLE

Around 1745–1818

Chicago is currently the third-largest city in the United States, but in the late 1700s it was a small community. For years and years, most people credited a white man as the city's founder. In reality, that man bought his land from a man named Jean Baptiste Point du Sable, who was Black.

Not much is known about du Sable's early life before the 1770s. He was of African descent, and is believed to have been born to a French father and an enslaved African woman in the 1740s. His exact birthplace is unknown, but most people think he was born on the island now known as Haiti. He made his way to North America, and after living in a few different places, he put down roots near the shore of Lake Michigan in Illinois. A letter from a British army officer in 1779 described du Sable as "a handsome negro, well educated, and settled at Eschikagou (Chicago)." He probably spoke French and most likely was a Catholic.

Du Sable wasn't the first person to live in the area we now call Chicago. For thousands of years, indigenous people, mostly Algonquins, had made this area around the Great Lakes their home. Then in the late 1600s, French traders arrived and trekked back and forth through the area, hunting and gathering other natural resources to sell or trade.

Du Sable was, however, the first non-Native American permanent settler in the area, and he represented the multiracial, multicultural reality that has always been true of what became the United States. In 1788, du Sable married a Native American woman of the Potawatomi people. Her name was Kitihawa, but Europeans called her by the name she took when she became a Christian—Catherine. Together, she and du Sable had two children and even a grandchild who was born in the Chicago area. Kitihawa's status as an indigenous person made it possible for du Sable to settle in the Chicago area and to thrive as a business-person. She was able to help him set up strong relationships with the local tribes, who then agreed to buy and trade with him.

Du Sable lived in the Chicago area for nearly twenty years, be-tween about 1780 and 1800. He is most known as a very successful entrepreneur—someone who starts their own businesses. When du Sable eventually moved away from Chicago, a receipt from when he sold his property shows that he owned a cabin, farmland, a bakery, a dairy to milk cows, a smokehouse to preserve meat, a stable for horses, and two barns. He was able to do all of this in a time when the whole area was mostly woods, hardly any non-Native Americans lived there, and there was not an established European or colonial business mar-ket. This meant that du Sable had to be very good at spotting potential opportunities to make money and build businesses.

It is important for us to remember Jean Baptiste Point du Sable because the presence of a successful Black entrepreneur so early in our nation's history tells us that people of African descent had all the cre-ativity, toughness, and skill necessary for "life, liberty, and the pursuit of happiness." Du Sable and his family show that people only need an opportunity. Du Sable had an advantage that other Black people of his time did not have because he lived in a land that did not have many Europeans, and he could live as a free person instead of as a slave. His marriage meant that he had friends in the local indigenous population who could help him.

As important as du Sable was to the founding of Chicago, he remained largely unknown for a long time because he was Black. That's because many white people in the United States did not want to recognize the ways Black people contributed to the founding of this nation. Doing that would mean admitting that Black people had equal abilities, skills, and potential as white people, and that fact makes it harder to subject Black people to slavery and other kinds of injustice.

Du Sable died in 1818 in St. Charles, Missouri, where he moved after he left Chicago. But respect for him as an entrepreneur with a multicultural family, and as an adventurous settler, is growing by the year.

BENJAMIN BANNEKER

1731–1806

Have you ever written a letter to an elected official such as a mayor, governor, or president? Letter writing is an important part of living in a democracy because it's one of the ways politicians hear from the people they are supposed to represent. This has been true of American democracy since the country began, and it's the tool a Black man named Benjamin Banneker used to push for Black freedom and fight for justice. But writing important letters is just one part of Banneker's incredible background.

Benjamin Banneker never personally knew the misery of being enslaved. His parents were free, and they owned a tobacco farm in Baltimore County, Maryland, where he was born in 1731. Banneker received an informal education from his family and his grandmother, who was a white woman and former indentured servant. In 1771, the Ellicots—a white Quaker family in Pennsylvania—moved near the Banneker's farm. Banneker and George Ellicot struck up a friendship. Ellicot would lend Banneker books and lunar tables to use for astronomy. He became a sort of personal librarian for Banneker in a time when Black people usually didn't have access to books and education.

Banneker loved to learn, and he quickly mastered the material he was reading. He was so brilliant that in 1752, he was able to borrow a watch, take it apart to see how it worked, and build a different watch made up entirely of wooden parts. It is said to be the first clock made in America and it accurately kept time for decades.

He especially loved mathematics and astronomy. Later in his life, Banneker started writing books called almanacs that contained information about weather patterns, the position of stars, and other facts. These almanacs he published from 1791 to 1802 became very popular and Banneker became well-known as a scientist and an intellectual. In 1790, he was even part of the team that conducted land surveys to plan for the new nation's capital, Washington, D.C.

Benjamin Banneker could have used the respect he gained as a scholar and a writer to build a life of comfort for himself. But he never forgot the hardship that other Black people faced. He knew he was part of a larger community of Black people, many of whom were enslaved. Instead of ignoring his brothers and sisters of African descent, he used his status and abilities to advocate on their behalf.

Banneker wrote a series of letters to Thomas Jefferson, who was the secretary of state at that time, to persuade him to work for Black freedom. In these letters, Banneker pointed to the Christian faith as a reason Jefferson should help abolish slavery. Banneker wrote about the equality of all people by talking about the Bible and writing, "[O]ne universal Father hath given being to us all, and that he hath not only made us all of one flesh," a statement tied to Acts 17:26. He didn't stop there. He argued that no matter a person's race or status, "we are all of the Same Family, and Stand in the Same relation to him [God]." He said that anyone who professes the "obligations of Christianity" ought to work for the uplift of all people.

Banneker then makes the letter personal for Thomas Jefferson by using Jefferson's own words against him to argue for Black emancipation. He wanted Jefferson to remember the time he "publickly held forth this true and invaluable doctrine . . . that all men are created equal." This showed Jefferson was not being true to his word. Banneker pointed out that in the Declaration of Independence, Jefferson wrote about equality and the right to freedom, but in real life, Jefferson enslaved hundreds of humans who were not free to pursue their own happiness.

Banneker also included a copy of his latest almanac in his letter. He wanted to show Jefferson that Black people were not less intelligent than white people and that they were capable of advanced scholarly work.

In a follow-up letter, Jefferson responded warmly to Banneker and thanked him for the almanac, though in the end Jefferson never really changed his ways. But Banneker's research and his work to liberate enslaved people was still important. Banneker's letter to Thomas Jefferson shows how Black people insisted they had the same level of gifts, abilities, and talents of white people because all humans were creations of God. Even in the early days of the United States, Black Christians tapped into the spirit of justice to protest their enslavement and show how it was nonsense to say you believe in Jesus and then also say it is acceptable to own fellow human beings.

The
ABOLITIONIST
MOVEMENT
1780–1870

The word *abolitionist* comes from the root word *abolish*, which means to "destroy" or "get rid of." So the abolitionist movement of the early 1800s was a movement to get rid of slavery in the United States. Frederick Douglass was one of the most prominent members of this movement. He did not like hypocrites, especially slaveholders who called themselves Christians and acted like anything but followers of Jesus Christ. Frederick was born enslaved in 1818, but he escaped to freedom as a young man in 1838, and went on to publish several autobiographies about his life under slavery. In his first book, he wrote about one of his enslavers, Thomas Auld. In 1832, Auld visited a Methodist camp meeting—a big outdoor church service that included several days of preaching. At that meeting, he became a Christian. Frederick wrote of his enslaver, "I indulged a faint hope that his conversion would lead him to emancipate his slaves, and that, if he did not do this, it would, at any rate, make him kinder and more humane. I was disappointed in both these respects." Not only did Christianity not make Auld a kinder human being or enslaver, if anything he became nastier. Douglass wrote that he turned "more cruel and hateful in all his ways; for I believe him to have been a much worse man after his conversion than before." All through his enslavement, Douglass came across white people who claimed to be Christian but enslaved Black people and treated them with cruelty.

At the end of his first book, Douglass had to make it clear to his readers that he had no problems with Christianity itself. He only disagreed with the kind of Christianity that slaveholders practiced.

Between the Christianity of this land, and the Christianity of Christ, I recognize the widest possible difference—so wide, that to receive the one as good, pure, and holy, is of necessity to reject the other as bad, corrupt, and wicked . . . I therefore hate the corrupt, slaveholding, women-whipping, cradle-plundering, partial and hypocritical Christianity of this land. Indeed, I can see no reason, but the most deceitful one, for calling the religion of this land Christianity.

Douglass, like so many other Black Christians, knew the difference between the Christianity that Jesus Christ taught and the religion of slaveholders. Many abolitionists were Christians too, but their view of religion argued against slavery rather than supporting it. All through the decades leading up to the Civil War in the 1860s, Black people and their white allies fought to make slavery and the slave trade illegal.

Slavery and the slave trade sound alike, but they are different. Slavery is the practice of enslaving people and forcing them to labor without pay. The slave trade is capturing people, putting them on ships, transporting them from place to place, and selling them for money or trading them for supplies. The slave trade became illegal in the United States in 1808, but slavery was still practiced until President Abraham Lincoln signed the Thirteenth Amendment in 1865.

But outlawing slavery was not easy, since it had become a big business, especially after Eli Whitney solved a major problem for cotton plantations. It took an enslaved person up to one full day to separate seeds from the fibers of one pound of cotton. Whitney invented the cotton gin (short for "engine") that quickly strained out the seeds.

Soon plantation owners all over the country were using the cotton gin. At the same time, the Industrial Revolution—the era when factories began producing large quantities of goods instead people making them all by hand—started to make its way into big cities in the US and Europe. Factories produced more products more quickly, which meant they needed more raw materials like cotton to keep production going. Soon the cotton industry was booming. But growing more cotton meant more enslaved people to plant, care for, and harvest it. Between 1790 and 1808—the year the slave trade was outlawed—US slaveholders transported eighty thousand Africans through the transatlantic slave trade. The number of slave states grew from six in 1790 to fifteen in 1860. By the start of the Civil War, nearly one in three people who lived in the South was an enslaved person.

But this boom in slavery was mostly in the South. The North had less open land for farming and was shifting to factories and industrial labor, so they did not need more enslaved people. In 1777, Vermont became the first state to abolish slavery outright. By 1804, all the northern states had passed laws to abolish slavery, at least gradually, in their territories. We should remember, however, that abolishing slavery in the North did not mean white people considered Black people equals. Racial prejudice and discrimination remained.

But Black people fought back with their faith. From the 1790s to the 1830s, a series of religious revivals took place throughout the country. Preachers would gather large crowds outside and preach to them. They warned and encouraged people to give their lives to Jesus and become "born again." This is the start of the evangelical movement in the US. In the Bible, the "evangel" is the good news about Jesus, who came to save sinners. Many revivals were open to both Black and white people. It also did not take any formal education or training to become a Christian or a preacher. So many Black people converted to Christianity.

When Black people became Christians, they made the religion their own. They looked at books in the Bible like Exodus and saw themselves in the story of God leading the Hebrew slaves out of Egypt and away from Pharoah's rule. They believed Jesus's words to "love your neighbor as yourself" and confronted white people with this teaching. They argued that because all people are made in God's image and likeness (Genesis 1:26–28), all human beings are equal and no one has the right to enslave another of God's children. Black Christians recognized in the life and example of Jesus the spirit of justice and tapped into that spirit to create the abolitionist movement.

PIERRE TOUSSAINT LOUVERTURE
1743–1803

No event before the Civil War inspired the spirit of justice among enslaved Africans more than the Haitian Revolution. It was the only slave rebellion that resulted in an independent, Black-led nation. Even though these Africans faced harsh consequences from white-majority countries including Britain and the United States, their successful, years-long effort to free themselves inspired Black people in the United States. Haiti stood as a proof that enslaved Africans could rebel against white enslavers and win.

The rebellion's leader was a Black man named Pierre Toussaint Louverture. He was born enslaved in 1743 and was legally freed in his thirties. At that time, Haiti was called St. Domingue and was a French slaveholding colony that produced mainly sugar and coffee. Louverture obtained some education through a Catholic group called the Jesuits. This led to his baptism and devout Christian faith.

In 1791, when Louverture was forty-eight, a slave revolt broke out, but at first he did not get involved. In fact, he helped his former master escape the island. But then Louverture joined the fight on the side of enslaved Africans in Haiti, and that's how his legend as the leader of the most successful slave rebellion in the Western hemisphere began.

The enslaved Haitians knew the land and the forests where they had been forced to work a lot better than the Europeans, and they used this to their advantage. Louverture trained his troops in guerilla (from the Spanish word *guerra*, which means "war") tactics that used fast-moving, small forces of men to make quick hit-and-run attacks. Even though they faced a superior military, Louverture was a brilliant military strategist, and his troops won many victories in battle.

A lot of people talk about Louverture as a military and government leader, but his faith played a big role in his life too. A lot of leaders force their religion on others and require people to worship the same god in the same way. But Louverture did not force Catholicism on the people as a national religion. He wanted every person to decide what they believed for themselves. "I would not jeopardize the sacred rights of conscience, so dear to every man, but grant all the privilege of worshipping God according to the dictates of their conscience." His example planted the seeds for religious freedom and tolerance in the new nation.

Louverture himself was a very spiritual man who practiced Catholicism as a sincere believer. An early slave record about him described him as "eager to proselytize [share his faith]." Documents show that he gave all of his children Christian names. He consistently expressed himself as a "devout Catholic during the Haitian Revolution." And it was largely because of his religious beliefs that Louverture recognized he and all African-descended people deserved freedom.

Louverture became a legend for helping lead Black people to freedom, but he was eventually captured during the revolution and imprisoned in 1802. Fearful of Louverture's leadership and brilliance in battle, French leaders invited him to a peaceful meeting to discuss "troop movements." But that was a lie. The French arrested him and forced him onto a ship headed for France. Once in prison, Louverture became sick, and he died in his cell in 1803. Before he died, he said, "In overthrowing me, you have cut down in San Domingo only the trunk of the tree of liberty. It will spring up again by the roots for they are numerous and deep." One man's death could not kill the spirit of justice.

In 1804, less than a year after Pierre Toussaint Louverture died, the Republic of Haiti became an independent nation and the first one formed out of a slave revolt. Enslaved Black people in North America would frequently look to Louverture as an example of resistance and courage. He showed that a slave rebellion could succeed even against an army that had more weapons and money. The desire for all Black people to have freedom became a reality in the Haitian Revolution. Now they had a real example of victory they could follow. Other Black leaders who led rebellions, such as Denmark Vesey and Nat Turner, would find inspiration in the way Louverture and his followers in Haiti fought against their enslavement.

DAVID WALKER
1796?–1830

The word radical *comes from an old Latin word that means "root." So a rad-*ical is someone who wants to move beyond simple solutions and get down to the root of a problem. In the nineteenth century, many times the word *radical* was used as a negative label for racial justice advocates who were willing to use any means necessary to gain freedom for themselves and others. Many white people thought David Walker was a radical.

Born in the 1790s to an enslaved father and a free Black mother, Walker was raised as a free person in Wilmington, North Carolina. He learned to read and write and traveled to many places when he was a young man. He eventually settled down in Boston, where he ran a clothing store.

Walker got labeled a "radical" because he wrote a controversial pamphlet called *Walker's Appeal, in Four Articles; Together with a Preamble, to the Coloured Citizens of the World, but in Particular and Very Expressly, to Those of the United States of America*—or just "Walker's Appeal" for short. His fiery words set the hearts of the enslaved—and the hair of slaveholders' heads—on fire.

"Oh! my coloured brethren, all over the world," Walker wrote, "when shall we arise from this death-like apathy?—And be men!!" Walker encouraged the masses of enslaved Black people to shake off the idea that they were meant for slavery and could not even protest. He pointed out that there were a lot more Black people than white people in slave states, and they had the numbers to quickly throw off their chains and drive out their slaveholders. In Walker's view, Black people had all they needed to secure freedom—the people, the strength, and the moral high ground. What they lacked was the will to make it happen.

The brief pamphlet was so packed with the potential for revolution that southern plantation owners banned it. When smugglers wanted to give out copies of the pamphlet in the South, sometimes they hid it by sewing its pages into the lining of their clothes.

While his words were often harsh, Walker was trying to show enslaved Black people their own power and their potential to fight for justice. His message was necessary for a people who had lived their entire lives under the slave driver's whip. The system of racial injustice was so complete that enslaved people almost never had an opportunity to hear a word about their God-given worth, their toughness, or the righteousness of their desire for freedom. Reading Walker's words told a people whose backs had been bent by slavery that it was alright to stand up straight and fight for their rights.

Some people thought that freedom for Black people in America meant going back to Africa. Walker was not one of those people. He saw going back to Africa—which was also called colonization—as another way white people could force Black people from their homes and opportunities. "Will any of us leave our homes and go to Africa? I hope not. America is more our country, than it is the whites—we have enriched it with our blood and tears." To Walker and many other Black people, the idea of sending formerly enslaved people who were born in the United States to the continent of Africa (where most of them had never been) was not an act of justice but of outrage. Black people had literally built the nation's wealth with the sacrifice of their bodies, lives, and loves. Now they were being told they could not remain in the land they had contributed so much to. Walker argued it would be better to stay in the United States and insist on being part of life in the only place they had ever known.

In the spirit of the Old Testament prophets, Walker insisted that white people turn from their wicked ways and seek justice for Black people and forgiveness from God. If they would not, prophesied Walker, then "I am awfully afraid that pride, prejudice, avarice and blood, will, before long, prove the final ruin of this happy republic, or land of liberty!!!!" While he could not have known the exact details of it, Walker predicted the coming of the Civil War. A nation could not claim to be the "land of liberty" while holding millions in slavery. Slavery and freedom cannot work together—people would have to takes sides, and one side would have to win.

David Walker's words were just that—words. They were not guns, knives, or bullets. Yet they had the power to kill ideas of Black inferiority or powerlessness. The words of his *Appeal* awakened the hopes, creativity, and courage of a people who had been told all their lives that they were less than white people. This message of positivity cut a small tear in the fabric of white supremacy that, if tugged on, might rip the entire lie apart. Oftentimes the most radical achievement does not start with actions but with words that powerfully remind people of their own worth and their ability to resist injustice.

ANNA MURRAY DOUGLASS

1813–1882

*You might have heard of Frederick Douglass. He was the most famous aboli-*tionist of the nineteenth century. He stands out as an individual with a tragic but exciting story of going from slavery to freedom, then writing about it in a world-famous book and becoming an international speaker. But Frederick Douglass could not have achieved all that he did on his own. This is the story of someone who is just as important to the history of Frederick Douglass, slavery, and freedom. This is the story of Anna Murray Douglass.

Anna Murray was born in Maryland around 1813. Her parents had been enslaved but were freed just one month before Anna was born, making her the first of their twelve children born into freedom. She left home at seventeen years old to support herself as a seamstress and domestic helper. Anna did not have the advantage of being taught how to read or write very well, but she excelled in management, financial planning, and resourcefulness.

Anna Murray met Frederick Bailey sometime in 1838 in Baltimore, perhaps while attending the same church. They fell in love, but the situation was difficult because Anna was free while Frederick was enslaved. Together, they hatched a plan for Frederick to escape with

Anna's help. First, she sewed a sailor's uniform. He would use that as a disguise and get on a train heading North to freedom. Next, Anna borrowed some "Freedom Papers"—documents that said a Black person was not enslaved and was not escaping. Frederick would show these papers as a kind of face ID so he could leave Maryland. The plan worked. Frederick made it to New York, and Anna joined him. She brought all the money and supplies they needed to start a new life. They were married in the home of an abolitionist, took the last name "Douglass," and settled in Massachusetts. Frederick Douglass, who became the most well-known abolitionist of the era, could not have escaped to freedom without Anna Murray's help.

Throughout their forty-four-year marriage, Anna Murray Douglass used her remarkable skills as an organizer and manager to run their household and give Frederick Douglass time for his public work. As he grew more famous, Anna Murray Douglass "in every possible way that she was capable of aided him by relieving him of all the management of the home as it increased in size and in its appointments." She provided for her husband by saving money and raising their five children, including a two-year stint when he was away on a speaking tour in Europe.

She also risked her life by taking Douglass in as a fugitive slave, for which she could have been arrested. Not until friends from England raised enough money in 1846 to legally purchase Douglass out of slavery did that danger pass. But even afterward, Anna Murray opened her home as a stop on the Underground Railroad to assist others escaping from slavery.

In all her efforts, Anna Murray Douglass professed faith in God and aspired to live a life that followed Jesus's example. Anna and Frederick were Methodists. Her daughter remembered their regular spiritual traditions: "Our custom was to read a chapter in the Bible around the table, each reading a verse in turn until the chapter was completed." This was not just meaningless routine for Anna Murray. "She was a person who strived to live a Christian life instead of talking it."

Anna Murray Douglass suffered a stroke in 1842 and died soon after. Even though we remember Frederick Douglass for his daring, his speeches, his writing, and his activism, he may never have made it out of slavery if not for the tireless efforts of his wife, Anna Murray. Certainly, his career as an abolitionist would not have been successful without her more than forty years of partnership. Anna Murray Douglass, through her unfailing strength and ability to work without recognition, exemplifies the spirit of justice. In 1900, Anna Murray's daughter, Rosetta Douglass Sprague, gave a speech and spoke about her mother. She explained that her father's story would not have been possible without her mother. "It was a story made possible through the unswerving loyalty of Anna Murray, to whose memory this paper is written." Unswerving loyalty in the cause of freedom is how Anna Murray Douglass lived out the spirit of justice.

PAUL CUFFE
1759–1817

Black nationalism is the idea that Black people should control their own money, politics, and communities. Some Black nationalists believe the only way for this to happen is for Black people to have their own country. One early Black nationalist was a man named Paul Cuffe (sometimes spelled Cuffee).

Cuffe was born in Massachusetts in 1759 to a formerly enslaved African father and a Native American mother, and was the seventh of ten children. His parents were able to save enough money to buy a 116-acre farm in Dartmouth, New Hampshire. But soon after his father died, the hard-working and independent Paul Cuffe left his life working the land for a life on the sea. He served on whaling ships, and during the Revolutionary War was captured by the British Navy and jailed for three months in New York.

After the war, Cuffe's justice work took many forms. In 1780, he and his brother John petitioned the Massachusetts legislature for the right to vote. They appealed to their Native American background to argue "that [we] are Indian men and by Law not the subjects of Taxation for any Estate Real or personal." The lawmakers did not approve their request, and later the brothers were briefly jailed for refusing to pay property taxes.

In the 1780s, Paul Cuffe partnered with a brother-in-law to start a shipping company. Cuffe recognized that Black people had to own their own businesses in order to gain true wealth. Instead of renting or sailing someone else's ships, he bought a small waterfront property and starting building ships for fishing and trade. Being a business owner allowed Cuffe and his coworkers to benefit in an area that had a growing population. More people meant more business and more money.

In time, Cuffe became one of the wealthiest Black people in the entire country.

But Cuffe was not happy just having a lot of money. He wanted to use his riches and position to help other Black people. He worked with a religious group called the Society of Friends (Quakers) in the United States and abolitionists in Britain to encourage formerly enslaved Black people from both nations to move to Sierra Leone—a colony started by England in 1791 to serve as a home for Black people who had joined with the British during the Revolutionary War.

Cuffe made several voyages to Sierra Leone to see if it would be a good place to settle formerly enslaved African Americans. After years of delay because of the War of 1812, Cuffe took a group of thirty-eight Black people to start a new life in Sierra Leone. Most of the cost for this journey fell on Cuffe, and this remarkable movement was only possible because of his financial wealth and the fact that he owned his own ships. Sierra Leone became a mix of indigenous Africans, formerly enslaved Africans from the US, and "maroons" from Jamaica who had fought in a failed slave rebellion and been deported.

While Cuffe had visionary plans for businesses and settlements for Black people in Sierra Leone, things mostly did not go as he had planned. The country was still a British colony, and British businessmen did not want the added competition of Black Americans coming to the country, buying land, and starting businesses of their own. In addition, the movement to bring Black people from United States back to Africa got a bad reputation because some people thought it was just a way for white people to get rid of Black people in the US.

Yet Paul Cuffe demonstrated there was power in Black people making money, and he showed that Black people were creative and courageous enough to imagine a nation for themselves. As a sailor, traveler, and business owner, Cuffe developed a vision of Black people from all over the globe uniting as one people and pictured a day when they all would be politically and financially independent. It was a vision ahead of its time. He held this dream all the way until his death in 1817.

Cuffe was a committed Christian and member of the Society of Friends. His faith drove his commitment to uplift his people. A good friend of his, Reverend Peter Williams Jr.—who pastored a church in New York City—said that Cuffe, was "[p]ious without ostentation, and warmly attached to the principles of Quakerism, he manifested, in all his deportment, that he was a true disciple of Jesus."

The
CIVIL WAR *and*
RECONSTRUCTION
1861–1877

There was only so long the United States could say it valued "life, liberty, and the pursuit of happiness" while also enslaving millions of Black people. The nation was bound to reach a breaking point between the forces of abolition and slavery. That breaking point came in the form of the Civil War.

On April 12, 1861, Confederate forces attacked Fort Sumter in South Carolina, officially beginning the Civil War. By this time, seven states had seceded—or withdrawn from the nation—and when fighting started in several more southern states, the entire South formed an alliance. They hoped they would become a new nation separate from the United States and called themselves the Confederate States of America (CSA).

A war never just breaks out. There are always events that build anger between groups until physical violence finally breaks out. Leading up to the Civil War, Christian communities broke apart before the states did. In 1844, northern and southern Methodists split because they disagreed about whether a bishop could perform his duties while also enslaving people. Methodists in the North said no while Methodists in the South said yes. As a result, the southern side separated from the northern Methodists and formed the Methodist Episcopal Church South (MECS) so they could practice both Christianity and slavery. In 1845, northern and southern Baptists split over the question of whether a Baptist missionary could go overseas and preach the gospel while still enslaving people in the US. Baptists in the North said no and Baptists in the South said yes. So the southern group split and formed their own denomination, the Southern Baptist Convention (SBC), which is still around today and is the largest Protestant denomination in the country. In 1861, southern Presbyterians joined the SBC and MECS by splitting from their northern brothers and sisters to form the Presbyterian Church of the Confederate States of America (PCCSA) and maintain the so-called "right" to enslave human beings.

In 1850, Congress passed the Fugitive Slave Act. This new law enraged Black people and northern white people. Enslavers in the South had a problem with enslaved people running away and escaping to freedom in non-slaveholding northern states. The Fugitive Slave Act said that Black "fugitives" who ran away from their plantations could be recaptured in the North and sent back down to their enslavers. This law basically made slavery a national practice, since it made no difference whether slavery was legal or illegal in a state—any Black person could be captured and sent back into slavery no matter where they were found. The law also made it illegal for anyone to help an escaped Black person.

But what finally made leaders in the South want to secede happened in 1860. That year Abraham Lincoln won the presidential election. Southerners saw Lincoln as an immediate threat to the practice of slavery. And while it is true that Lincoln thought slavery should be eliminated, that did not mean he thought Black people were equal with white people.

You may have heard that Lincoln "freed the slaves." There is more to the story. Lincoln did not oppose slavery because he had a great love of Black people, or because he wanted to help them. In 1862, a letter from Lincoln was published in the newspaper that read, "My paramount object in this struggle is to save the Union and is not either to save or to destroy slavery. If I could save the Union without freeing any slave I would do it, and if I could save it by freeing all the slaves I would do it." What was most important to Abraham Lincoln as president and commander in chief of the Union's armed forced was reuniting the states, not abolishing slavery. Lincoln eventually issued the Emancipation Proclamation in 1863, but the Union still had to win a bloody war before that could take effect.

Many white people, even in the North where slavery was already illegal, did not like Black people very much even if they agreed that slavery should be abolished in the South. At first, they did not want Black people fighting in the Civil War, even if it was for their own side. They believed racist lies that Black people were cowardly in battle and too unintelligent to lead white soldiers. That view eventually changed when the Union was losing and needed Black soldiers to help bail them out. Even then, Black soldiers were not usually promoted to high ranks or put on the front lines of battle. White commanders often assigned them tasks like digging ditches, building fortifications, and cooking.

White commanders in the Union also had an issue figuring out what they should do with the growing numbers of Black people who ran away to join the Union forces because they saw the war as their chance to escape slavery. Some military leaders returned Black people to their plantation owners. Others kept them as "contraband," or property captured in war. Since enslaved people were considered "property" already, legally they could be kept by Union forces so the Confederates could not use them for farming or military efforts.

Even with the discrimination they experienced from white Union soldiers and northerners, Black people still fought for the Union during the Civil War. They saw it as their chance to literally fight for their freedom. They led daring raids, faithfully served their fellow soldiers, and sacrificed their lives to attack the institution that had ruined so many of their lives. Black Christians saw the Civil War as a spiritual battle against the forces of good and evil, oppression and injustice. The war, as violent and deadly as it was, finally offered the possibility of liberty and the pursuit of happiness, and Black people entered the battle armed with the spirit of justice.

ROBERT SMALLS

1839–1915

Robert Smalls knew he could be killed if he got caught. But freedom was worth the risk. The Civil War had just started, and this was his best chance of leaving a life of bondage behind. So before sunrise on the morning of May 13, 1862, he went to steal a Confederate ship—his plan was to pick up his young family and several other enslaved Black people and then sail across Union lines; hopefully, toward emancipation. He wore a captain's hat as a disguise. He knew all the Confederate signals. He was also a good sailor who could steer the ship even in the dark. But would that be enough to get him and his passengers to safety?

Smalls was born enslaved in 1839 in Beaufort, South Carolina. Not all slavery involved picking cotton on a plantation. Smalls lived in a city and his labor, though still forced, was shaped by his environment. At twelve years old, Smalls's slaveholder loaned him out to work in the city of Charleston as a waiter in a hotel. Several years later, Smalls started laboring as a dockworker helping load and unload ships. During this time, he met and married his wife, Hannah, and they had two children.

Smalls worked his way up from dockworker to a crewmember who joined other sailors on ships. His slaveholder assigned him to a ship named the *Planter*, which was used to transport supplies for the

Confederacy during the war. Smalls learned quickly and became a "wheelman" who was trained to pilot the ship. He also paid attention to the white crewmembers in hopes of finding an opportunity for escape. Smalls noticed that the white crew often left the ship for the entire night to party or sleep somewhere else. As a result, the Black crewmembers were left alone on the ship for the whole night. That was their chance.

During the early hours in May 1862, Smalls gathered up a total of sixteen other enslaved men, women, and children to escape. He sailed through Confederate waters and into Union territory. Smalls knew the Union soldiers would only see a Confederate ship, and there was a risk they would fire on sight thinking their enemies were attacking. Which is why Smalls raised a white flag—the symbol of surrender in a war. Instead of sinking the boat, Union forces came on board and discovered the enslaved Black people. Smalls surrendered the ship and its cargo of artillery cannons, and the Union took all the passengers and freed them.

Stealing a Confederate ship and sailing it to freedom was bold, even by Civil War standards. Word of Robert Smalls's daring escape spread and made him an instant celebrity. Smalls could have simply enjoyed being famous and lived a life of comfort and safety. But he continued to fight for freedom by joining the Union's navy. He was such a good sailor that his commanders promoted him to captain and gave him command of his own ships. After a while, the navy even put him in command of the *Planter*, the ship he had stolen from the Confederates. Smalls and his family eventually saved enough money to go back to Charleston after the war and purchase his former enslaver's mansion. He now owned the house of the man who had once owned him.

After his escape, a white Methodist minister with the American Missionary Association arrived in Charleston. He heard about Smalls's story and recruited him to help raise money for the Port Royal Experiment—an ambitious government program to support formerly enslaved people. Their first fundraising trip was to Washington, D.C., to give a speech in front of 1,200 people at a church. Smalls had never given a speech in front of a crowd before. Many people would have frozen or run away in fear. But Smalls had faced much greater dangers in his life. People loved hearing him speak. His story was so powerful that he immediately received more invitations to share it and went on to give many, many more speeches to huge audiences.

Smalls was a Christian, and his faith played a role in his work after the Civil War ended. He helped draft South Carolina's new state constitution and served as an elected official, first as a state representative and senator and then as a US congressman. He also served in South Carolina's state militia and rose to the rank of brigadier general. But as racists rose to political power, they attacked him with lies and accusations until they tanked his political career. In the face of this slander, Smalls wrote in 1909, "But notwithstanding all this, the same God still lives, in whom we place our hope."

When he died in 1915, a service was held at First African Baptist Church in Charleston, where he had been a member for ten years. It was said to have been "the largest ever held in the city." Throughout his life, Smalls displayed a bravery and willingness to battle racism and white supremacy in a way that made his memory a part of national history. From slave to Civil War hero and general, to statesman and celebrity—Smalls was empowered by the spirit of justice. He lived by his own words: "My race needs no special defense, for the past history of them in this country proves them to be equal of anyone. All they need is an equal chance in the battle of life."

The EMANCIPATION PROCLAMATION *and* JUNETEENTH

January 1, 1863 and June 19, 1865

Nearly two years into the Civil War, Abraham Lincoln signed the Emancipation Proclamation. (*Emancipation* means "freedom," and a proclamation is an announcement.) Most people think the Emancipation Proclamation "freed the slaves," but even though that isn't exactly true, it was still an important document.

By the summer of 1862, the Civil War was fully underway, and everyone was asking what the president would do about slavery. Would he abolish it or try to compromise with the Confederates in order to get them to rejoin the Union? Lincoln was not passionate about Black emancipation, and he actually supported a plan to ship Black people back to Africa instead of allowing them to live freely in the United States. Two of Lincoln's military commanders had already issued their own versions of an emancipation proclamation because they were on the front lines of war and had to figure out what to do about the enslaved people they came across who wanted to join them. But Lincoln withdrew those proclamations almost immediately. Eventually, though, the war forced Lincoln to rethink his position. Black people kept running away from the South to cross into Union territory in the hope of finding freedom. White and Black abolitionists were pressuring politicians to outlaw slavery. Finally, Lincoln decided to make the proclamation. "I do order and declare that all persons held as slaves within said designated States, and parts of States, are, and henceforward shall be free," the proclamation said. It also allowed Black people to be "received into the armed service of the United States." That meant Black people could officially become soldiers for the Union. But the proclamation had limits.

The Emancipation Proclamation did not end slavery. The Thirteenth Amendment, which was passed in January 1865, is what actually abolished slavery in the United States. The Emancipation Proclamation only freed some enslaved people—the ones in Confederate territories that had not yet been taken over by the Union. It left slavery in the border states—Missouri, Kentucky, West Virginia, Maryland, and Delaware—untouched. (These states supported slavery but they didn't join the Confederacy, so they were still considered part of the Union.) And the Emancipation Proclamation would not go into effect until January 1, 1863. On top of that, the proclamation would mean nothing unless the Union won the Civil War, and at the time it wasn't clear that would happen.

After the announcement, Lincoln made this statement: "I can only trust in God I have made no mistake . . . It is now for the country and the world to pass judgment on it." Lincoln understood the gravity of the Emancipation Proclamation both for the war effort and for the nation.

There was even a proclamation before the Emancipation Proclamation. It was called the Compensated Emancipation Act, and it was just for Washington, D.C., the Union capital. They passed it because slavery was still legal in D.C., and it didn't make sense for the Union to be fighting against slavery while people still practiced it in the capital. *Compensated* means "paid." Since slaves were considered property, the government actually paid slaveholders $300 for each enslaved person they freed. It paid just $100 to each freed person, and only if they agreed to leave the country and move back to Africa.

For Black Christians in the South, the time between the announcement of the Emancipation Proclamation in 1862 and when it went into effect in January 1863 was one of hope and anxiety. Would Lincoln follow through? Would there be a last-minute compromise? Would Black people finally be free? Black people took their requests and fears to God, and they waited.

Finally, just after midnight on December 31, 1862, messengers from the telegraph office carried the news. Freedom! The celebration was unbelievable. Black people "got into such a state of enthusiasm that almost everything seemed to be witty and appropriate to the occasion." But some enslaved people did not hear about the Emancipation Proclamation until years later. The people in Galveston, Texas, did not know about the proclamation until June 19, 1865—more than two years after it went into effect. Ever since then, Black people have celebrated June 19th—Juneteenth—as Emancipation Day. It is the oldest celebration of Black freedom from slavery in the country. In 2021, President Joe Biden signed a bill that made Juneteenth a national holiday so all people can celebrate the abolition of slavery.

Black Christians understood the struggle for liberation as a spiritual war between slavery and freedom. Through constant standing up for their rights, years of abolitionist organizing, and an unfailing hope that God would free them just like the Hebrew slaves from Egypt, Black people drew on the spirit of justice to make the dream of freedom a reality.

HARRIET TUBMAN
1821 or 1822–1913

When she died in 1913, Harriet Tubman was known as the "Moses of her people." She had become famous as a "conductor" on the Underground Railroad—which wasn't really a railroad, but a network of abolitionists who helped escaping slaves by hiding them and guiding them on the way to freedom up North. Tubman, who was born enslaved and escaped to the North, went back down South a total of thirteen times and helped lead more than seventy enslaved people to freedom. Most people know Harriet Tubman for these daring journeys, but what many people do not know is that Harriet Tubman was also a spy and a leader in the Civil War.

She was born around 1821 to enslaved parents, who named her Araminta Ross. When she grew up, she married a man named John Tubman and took her mother's first name, Harriett. Life in slavery was often very cruel, and Tubman later recounted that she'd received a permanent head injury as a young woman. Her slaveholder ordered her to tie up another enslaved person for a whipping. Tubman refused. The slaveholder then threw a heavy item—perhaps a rock or a piece of metal—at the other enslaved person, but it hit Tubman instead and fractured her skull. After the injury, she would sometimes fall into a sudden, deep sleep, almost like being in a coma, for brief periods. In these moments she saw visions from the Lord about dangers to avoid and missions that God had for her.

In 1849, Tubman decided she would be free. She self-liberated herself by escaping from her plantation at night and making her way to the North. Doing this was unsafe for anyone, but it was especially difficult for Black women, who also had parents and children to take care of on top of their duties on the plantation. Tubman left her husband—who did not want to risk the danger—and the rest of her family behind. But as soon as she made it to freedom, she resolved that if she was free, the rest of her family ought to be free as well. That's when she started making trips back to plantations to guide other enslaved people to freedom through the Underground Railroad.

By the time the Civil War began, Tubman was already a well-known figure. In 1862, Massachusetts's governor, John Andrew, arranged for Tubman to travel to South Carolina and help the Union military efforts there.

She served wherever she could and displayed a remarkable ability to get things done. She helped provide food, clothing, and supplies to soldiers at the fort; she trained women to wash clothes, bake, and make their own money; and she helped as a nurse, taking care of the soldiers and freed people who got sick from the many diseases working their way through the camp. After the Emancipation Proclamation, Tubman had great success recruiting Black soldiers, since they now had official permission to join the Union.

But Tubman wanted to be closer to the front lines, where she could help even more. She had firsthand experience with slavery, knew about the land and trails, and as a Black woman, she could get updates from other Black people that white Union soldiers couldn't receive. On July 2, 1863, Tubman became the first woman to plan and lead an armed mission during the Civil War.

Under cover of night, Tubman guided three hundred Union soldiers on steamships in the Combahee River. They went ashore and hunted down Confederate soldiers, then signaled to Black people in the area that they could join up with Union forces and gain their freedom. At first slowly, then in a rush, the enslaved Black people ran toward the river and the Union steamships waiting there. There were so many people that the boats almost sank from overcrowding.

Desperate for order, a white Union leader looked to Tubman for help. After standing silently for several minutes, Tubman began singing. The tune caught on and soon the escaping Black people joined in. The effect was calming, and the evacuation continued in a swift and orderly manner. By the time morning came, over seven hundred Black people had been liberated from slavery. Tubman was able to free more Black people in one night than in ten years of trips back and forth to the South.

Harriet Tubman defied tradition, law, and expectations to become the "Moses of her People." Like the Hebrews in the book of Exodus, her courageous adventures cannot be understood apart from her faith in God. With her faith and her selfless dedication to Black freedom, Tubman had the spiritual resources to fight for freedom.

When she died, Tubman was given a full military burial in recognition of her service to the Union. Her bravery during the Civil War made her both a hero and a patriot. Tubman displayed boldness in her efforts to free slaves because she believed the spirit of justice was within her and guided her actions.

ELIZABETH KECKLEY

1818–1907

Making a difference in the world doesn't always look like fighting wars or making big speeches. Elizabeth Keckley used her eye for fashion and skill with a needle to literally sew her way into history. Born into slavery in 1818 in Virginia, she went on to become a famous dressmaker in Washington, D.C., and served President Lincoln's wife, Mary Todd Lincoln, in the White House.

Much of what we know about Keckley is from the autobiography she wrote about her life. Growing up, she never knew her father but believed he was an enslaved Black man. In reality, her biological father was a white man named Armistead Burwell, the man who enslaved her and her mother. Burwell sent her away to North Carolina to work for his son, Robert Burwell.

Robert Burwell treated Keckley harshly. Encouraged by his wife, Burwell let another white man severely whip Keckley with a leather strap for her "stubborn pride." Keckley refused to let out even a scream as the man whipped her. The man then tried to beat her again, but each time he attempted, Keckley fought with him even though he was stronger. The third time he tried to hurt her, she wore him down. "As I stood bleeding before him, nearly exhausted with his efforts, he burst into tears, and declared that it would be a sin to beat me anymore." Robert Burwell tried to beat her in the weeks following, but Keckley again resisted. Keckley would not give up and simply accept her torture, so even a man as cruel as Burwell had to see that she was not a piece of property but a human being. Burwell finally told her, "with an air of penitence, that he should never strike me another blow; and faithfully he kept his word." Keckley noted in her writings that Burwell was a pastor and the other man who beat her went to his church.

Keckley continued to suffer after she left her half brother's house. He sent her to another man who was even more cruel—he assaulted her throughout the four years she labored in his household. She wrote, "I was regarded as fair for one of my race . . . I do not care to dwell upon this subject, for it is one that is fraught with pain." Keckley was ultimately forced to have the man's child, her only son, George, who would later die in the Battle of Wilson's Creek in 1861 after joining the Union Army and passing as a white man.

Elizabeth Keckley was a domestic servant in white slaveholders' homes. You might think that laboring in a house would be easier than laboring in the fields. But even though household slaves did not have the same backbreaking work in the heat of the sun that field slaves did, they still had a hard life. Household labor in the 1800s was difficult work. Washing clothes, cooking multiple meals a day, bringing in firewood, emptying trash, and taking care of the children was exhausting. And you had to work with the slaveholder watching your every move. Every mistake was in plain sight. Plus, women also had to deal with the demands of the male plantation owner's wife, many of whom were jealous and upset that another woman was in the house. Yet Keckley resisted by rising above her circumstances.

After Armistead Burwell died, Keckley was sent to serve the joint household of his widow and her daughter (Keckley's half sister, Anne Garland), and became a seamstress to help bring in money for her slaveholders. For a time she supported the entire household, including her slaveholders, through her work. After several years in their household,

Keckley asked to purchase her and her son's freedom. Keckley had no money of her own and had made plans to visit New York and beg abolitionists there for money to buy her freedom. But before she left, a white woman who Keckley had made dresses for and who had developed a friendship with her offered to raise the money among the other white people Keckley had made dresses for. They were able to get the money and in 1855, Keckley bought freedom for herself and her son.

Finally free, Elizabeth Keckley made her way to Washington, D.C. Even though there were still many racist people in that city, she was able to start a dressmaking business there. The ladies who paid for her services liked her and kept recommending Keckley to their friends. Soon she was making dresses for the rich and famous people in town. For a while her best customer was Varina Davis, the wife of Jefferson Davis, who would later become the president of the Confederacy. She also sewed for Mary Custis Lee, wife of Robert E. Lee, before he joined the Confederacy and became its most famous general. A customer even introduced Keckley to Mary Todd Lincoln shortly after Abraham was elected president, and the two began a long and close relationship.

But Keckley had concerns beyond sewing fabric and making dresses. One warm August evening, Keckley and a friend were taking a stroll when she heard music. Following the sound, she found it was coming from a party to raise money for hospitals. She thought to herself, "If the white people can give festivals to raise funds for the relief of suffering soldiers, why should not the well-to-do colored people get to work to do something for the benefit of the suffering blacks?"

The next Sunday at her church, Union Bethel, she suggested to the congregation that they form a relief society. Within a couple of weeks, she was president of the Contraband Relief Association and overseeing forty volunteers. Keckley used her connections to famous people, which included Frederick Douglass and Henry Highland Garnett, and her relationship with Mary Todd and Abraham Lincoln to raise money to help newly freed Black people. After the Emancipation Proclamation, the association changed its name to the Ladies' Freedmen and Soldier's Relief Association.

Women such as Elizabeth Keckley who, through years of hard labor, had secured their own freedom and economic stability saw it as their duty to assist others of their race. Keckley carefully navigated Black and white social circles to raise funds and other forms of support for the Ladies Freedmen and Soldier's Relief Association. Keckley tapped into the spirit of justice by effectively using her skills as a business owner, dressmaker, and style icon to help lift her people just as they were gaining their freedom from slavery.

The

JIM CROW ERA

1877 to late 1960s

After the Civil War, Black people enjoyed the sunshine of freedom. For a short time from about 1865 to 1877, they experienced a period called "Reconstruction." They built schools to finally get a formal education, they ran for political office for the first time, they built Christian organizations and denominations. But all of that came to a swift end with the compromise of 1877. After a very close presidential election, southern politicians agreed to give the Rutherford B. Hayes the presidency if he agreed to withdraw all federal troops from the South. The government troops were there to make sure that new laws protecting Black people were followed. Once they were removed, Black people were left to the cruelties of southerners who had lost the war but not their racial prejudice. Even in the North, Black people faced discrimination. Many people in the nation had not given up their ideas about white superiority and Black inferiority.

From the late 1800s through the 1960s, the United States was stuck in a period called the Jim Crow era. The phrase "Jim Crow" comes from the name of a minstrel character played by a white man named Thomas D. Rice in the 1830s. Rice used "blackface"—painting your face dark to look like a Black person—in his plays. He pretended to be a trickster named Jim Crow who was likable, but also foolish, clumsy, and poor. The character and others like it were meant to make fun of Black people. After the Civil War, many white people remembered the character and thought that it correctly described Black people. So they started to call this time period the Jim Crow era.

During Jim Crow in 1846, the United States Supreme Court ruled in a case called *Plessy v. Ferguson*. This trial was about whether a Black man named Homer Plessy could legally ride in a train car reserved for white people. Plessy and his lawyers argued for "equal treatment under the law" for Black people. But the Supreme Court disagreed. They said forcing racial separation was just fine and did not mean that Black people were not equal to white people. White people forced Black people to go to separate schools, live in separate neighborhoods, use separate doors, drink from separate drinking fountains, and exist separate from white people in as many ways as possible. White people kept all the money and resources for their own schools, businesses, and neighborhoods, and left Black people with hardly anything. This era was separate but certainly not equal.

As if this was not enough, the Jim Crow era was also a time when lynching became tragically common. A lynching is when someone is killed without a trial or a conviction. In the United States, lynching was a form of terrorism used to scare Black people and force them to follow racist polices like segregation. This is also the time when organizations such as the Ku Klux Klan grew and spread around the country.

Emmett Till was just fourteen years old when he was lynched in Mississippi in 1955. He lived in Chicago, but he was spending the summer with relatives in the South. One day, he and some other teenagers went to Bryant's Grocery and Meat Market to buy a snack. Emmett was accused of whistling at or touching the hand of a white woman named Carolyn Bryant while he was in the store. In those days, a Black man could get in serious trouble if they showed any interest in a white woman—or even seemed like they had. Bryant told her husband, and later that night he and his brother-in-law kidnapped Emmett from his relatives' home. They severely beat him, shot him, then strapped a seventy-five-pound metal fan around his ankles with barbed wire and dumped him in the Tallahatchie River. We know about Emmett Till because when they found his body, his mother, Mamie Till-Mobley, insisted that magazines show his horribly disfigured face. Her brave and painful decision to let the world see the reality of racist lynchings and helped spark the civil rights movement.

Segregation and racist violence mark the era of Jim Crow, but other events were happening as well. Black people did not give up fighting for justice, and in this new period of freedom they resisted in a way they never could have under slavery. Black people built institutions. They started churches, denominations, colleges, banks, businesses, newspapers, and more. William J. Simmons put it this way: "Untrammeled, we have, out of our ignorance and penury, built thousands of churches, started thousands of schools, educated millions of children, supported thousands of ministers of the Gospel, organized societies for the care of the sick and the burying of the dead." With remarkable speed and skill, Black people drew on the spirit of justice to craft lives they could only pray and dream about when they were enslaved.

ELIAS CAMP MORRIS

1855–1922

Sometimes we don't remember the names of people who lived remarkable lives, but their work lives on through the organizations they built. That's the case with Elias Camp Morris, the first president of the National Baptist Convention—the largest Black Christian denomination in the United States. Many people have not heard of Rev. Morris, but his leadership of this religious body continues to have an impact today.

After the Civil War, Black people couldn't wait to use their newfound freedom to start building a new world for themselves. One of the first things they did was form their own religious groups. Under slavery, many Black Christians had been treated like second-class citizens in church—the household of God. After emancipation, however, Black people rushed to select their own pastors, build their own churches, and form their own congregations. Over time, these groups organized into networks of churches called denominations, and E. C. Morris was one of the first and most important Black denominational leaders after the Civil War.

Elias Camp Morris was born enslaved in Georgia in 1855. Not a lot of Black people at that time could get a college education, but he did. He went to Nashville Normal and Theological Institute (now Roger

Williams University). He felt the call to be a minister early in his life and Baptists licensed him to preach when he was nineteen. Like a lot of other Black people in the decades after emancipation, Morris headed west for more opportunities than he found in the Deep South. He was on his way to Kansas when he made a stop at the small town of Helena, Arkansas, right on the banks of the Mississippi River in a region called the Delta. Samuel Clemens—also known as Mark Twain, the author of *Adventures of Huckleberry Finn* and other books—wrote in his memoirs that Helena "occupies one of the prettiest situations on the Mississippi." Morris may have agreed, because instead of continuing to Kansas, he settled down in Helena and spent the rest of his life there.

Morris had a college education and was a really good preacher. Plus, he was excellent at organizing and leading groups of people. So in 1879, the people of Centennial Baptist Church ordained him as their pastor. At first, they just had a small building, but with Morris as their pastor the congregation grew from twenty-three people to more than one thousand. As a result, they raised some money and built a new, big, beautiful church, which was designed by a Black man named Henry James Price and opened in 1905. It was constructed with red bricks, it had two towers on the corners of the building, stunning stained-glass windows, and could seat one thousand people. The church became a meeting place where Black people would hold church services, funerals, meetings, and special events.

There were a lot of small Baptist organizations at the time, and it was clear they could do more together than apart. After lots of talking, leaders of the different groups decided to form one large group and call it the National Baptist Convention. But they needed a strong leader, someone with organizational skills and visionary dreams, who was also rooted in the Black community and had the respect of both Black and white people. Elias Camp Morris was the man for the job, and he served as president of the NBCUSA, Inc. from 1895 until he died in 1922.

Leading the new denomination wasn't easy. One of Morris's greatest challenges came toward the end of his life during Red Summer of

1919. On September 30, Black sharecroppers near the town of Elaine, Arkansas, gathered in a rickety old church to figure out how to get fair prices for they cotton they had picked that season. Getting this money could lift them out of poverty and open new possibilities. But the Black farmers knew that having a meeting like this would make white people mad, so they set armed guards outside the church to keep watch.

Sure enough, that night a group of white men showed up to the meeting. A shootout started. One of the white men was wounded and another was killed. Early the next day, intentionally misleading newspaper headlines read, "Negro insurrection!" Hundreds of white people from Arkansas, Tennessee, and Mississippi flooded into the Elaine area. Over the next two days, they hunted down and shot almost any Black person they could find. It took Army troops to finally stop the violence, and the soldiers themselves may have also killed some Black people. To this day, we do not know the exact number of Black people killed in the "Elaine Massacre," but historians estimate that the white mob murdered up to two hundred people. Morris helped lead the community after the shock of this massacre. He comforted the many members of his congregation who had friends or family killed in the events. He also helped make sure that innocent Black people did not get convicted in court for crimes they did not commit during the riot.

By the time Morris died in 1922 after an extended illness, he had led the largest organization of Black people in the country for nearly thirty years. His legacy stands as one of the clearest examples of how a Black pastor was more than just a preacher—he was a community leader. He used his skills in business, politics, and preaching to uplift his people. Even as he fought racism, Morris expressed the spirit of justice by building a Black organization—the National Baptist Convention—into a community that has lasted nearly 130 years.

WILLIAM J. SEYMOUR

1870–1922

In the Bible, Pentecost is the day when the Holy Spirit came down from heaven and rested on the disciples fifty days after Easter. The Spirit gave Jesus's followers the power to "speak in tongues," or languages they had never learned (Acts 2:1–13). But the Spirit did more than grant gifts—it brought unity to the people of God. And much, much later, William J. Seymour used the Holy Spirit to unite Black and white Christians.

William J. Seymour was born in Louisiana in 1870, part of the first generation of Black people born after the abolition of slavery. As a young man, Seymour came down with smallpox, and it left him blind in one eye. But Seymour still had vision, a spiritual kind. He moved to Indiana and learned about the idea of radical holiness—that the Holy Spirit would make a person completely holy after they committed to Christ. That led him to Houston, Texas, in 1903, where he met a man named Charles Fox Parham. Seymour took classes about the Holy Spirit from Parham, but Jim Crow laws meant that Black students could not be in the same class with white students. So Seymour sat in the hallway and listened to lectures from outside.

Seymour learned about the baptism of the Holy Spirit and the gift of speaking in tongues from Parham. Pentecostals like Seymour believed that you had to be "baptized" by the Holy Spirit, and the proof of your faith was that you could speak in tongues. In 1906, a church in Los Angeles invited Seymour to help pastor there, and he began preaching about the baptism of the Holy Spirit and speaking in tongues.

Not everyone agreed with Seymour, and the head pastor kicked him out of their meetings. Seymour fasted and prayed for a month and then began preaching from the front porch of a friend's home. The crowds who came to hear him soon overcrowded the small house, and they had to move the services to an abandoned African Methodist Episcopal Church on Azusa Street. For three years, from 1906 to 1909, Seymour and his team led the Azusa Street Revival—it was the birth of the modern Pentecostal movement.

Thousands of visitors and worshipers gathered for services three times a day, seven days a week. Hundreds of people packed into a small room and prayed for the gifts of the Spirit. At any time, a person could begin speaking in tongues or start shouting or dancing, caught up in the presence of God.

Los Angeles was the perfect setting for a multiracial revival. It was a city that brought together white people, Black people, Native Americans, Mexican Americans, Europeans, and Asian immigrants. People of many races, nations, and ethnicities came to the revival on Azusa Street. A journalist at the time wrote, "The color line was washed way in the blood [of Jesus Christ]."

But Parham, Seymour's mentor and the man who helped him get to California, did not support Seymour after learning of what was happening at the revival. He visited Los Angeles in October 1906 and did not like the interracial mixing at the revival. Parham believed that God had created white people as the superior race and that having children with so-called inferior races like Black people was the cause of all kinds of disasters and sicknesses. He seemed to support the racist Ku Klux Klan group, he called Black people bad names, and in his publication, *Apostolic Faith*, he frequently published racist articles.

Seymour and other Pentecostals, however, continued to promote racial unity in the Holy Spirit. In his "Doctrines and Disciplines of the Azusa Street Mission of Los Angeles, California," Seymour wrote, "We want all of our white brethren and white sisters to feel free in our churches and missions." He viewed this movement toward racial reconciliation as a sign of Jesus Christ at work in the church. "Jesus Christ takes in all people in his salvation. Christ is all and for all. He is neither black nor white man, nor Chinaman, nor Hind[u], nor Japanese, but God. God is a Spirit, because without his spirit we cannot be saved."

Over time Pentecostals organized themselves into denominations. At first, they had both Black and white members, but they soon split along racial lines. To this day, Pentecostal churches and denominations struggle to unite across races. These churches separated by race are a long way off from the beginnings of the Pentecostal movement. A pastor named Herbert Daughtry said about Seymour and the early Pentecostal church, "Perhaps the greatest miracle was that color and class lines were broken down. Everybody was the same."

The example of the Azusa Street Revival and the early Pentecostal movement demonstrates that a focus on the Holy Spirit creates space for all different kinds of people to come together. By focusing on a meeting with God through the Spirit, Pentecostals briefly experienced the reality of Galatians 3:28: "There is neither Jew nor Gentile, neither slave nor free, nor is there male and female, for you are all one in Christ Jesus." While the diversity of Pentecostalism did not last, this interracial cooperation is an example of how the spirit of justice helped bring racial unity to the church.

ANNA JULIA COOPER

1858–1964

If you want to travel to another country, you'll need a passport. In every passport booklet issued by the United States government, you can read this sentence: "The cause of freedom is not the cause of a race or a sect, a party or a class—it is the cause of humankind, the very birthright of humanity." This quote is by Anna Julia Cooper, and putting her words in an official government document is one way that people have honored her remarkable life.

Cooper was born into slavery in 1858 in Raleigh, North Carolina, and lived to be 105 years old. Cooper's mother was enslaved, and her father was probably her slaveholder's brother—although Anna's mother never confirmed this with her. Unlike many other enslaved women at the time, Anna gained a formal education at early age and took advantage of her academic opportunities. She went to St. Augustine's Normal and Collegiate Institute in Raleigh and did very well as a student there. When she graduated at eighteen, she married a classmate, George Cooper, who had trained to be a minister. Sadly, George died only two years later. For the rest of her life, Anna remained single and committed her time and energy to education.

Cooper enrolled in Oberlin College, a school well-known for its ties to abolitionism before the Civil War and for being one of the few colleges open to Black students at the time. To call Anna Julia Cooper an "A" student would be an understatement. She was brilliant. She had done so well in high school that she skipped freshman year and started college as a sophomore. After she graduated, Cooper kept getting more education. She went on to earn a master's degree from Oberlin in 1887.

Cooper then moved to Washington, D.C., accepted a teaching position at the prestigious M Street High School, which was later renamed Paul Lawrence Dunbar High School, the same school Charles Hamilton Houston attended a bit later—you'll learn more about Houston further in the book. She eventually became principal of the school. Cooper believed that Black people could and should learn advanced academic subjects such as Latin, Greek, French, and philosophy just as she had. She used her ideas to make M Street High School into a feeder school that helped students attend universities such as Harvard and Yale. But some white people didn't like the idea of Black people getting such advanced education, and Cooper was dismissed from her job.

Cooper used this setback as an opportunity to fulfill a lifelong dream: she earned her PhD. It took her more than ten years, but she finally graduated with a doctorate in philosophy from the Sorbonne in Paris in 1925. She was sixty-six years old! She became just the fourth Black woman to earn a PhD. In 1931, Cooper became the president of Frelinghuysen University in Washington, D.C., a non-traditional school serving working adult, Black learners that became a model for the modern community college system.

Cooper is best known for writing a book of essays called *A Voice from the South*. In this book, she wrote about women's education, racial conflicts, and the Episcopal church, where she was a member. The book was published in 1892, and established Cooper as a world-class scholar and an example for other women for generations to come.

Even in her academic work, Cooper's Christianity played a role. She defined faith simply as "treating the truth as true." For her, no one lived this principle of faith more than Jesus Christ. "His faith was . . . an optimistic vision of the human aptitude for endless expansion and perfectibility." Cooper's ideas about education were partly shaped by her understanding of Jesus's life. Just like Christ lived as a person of limitless possibility, Cooper believed that all people could endlessly improve their moral, social, and intellectual abilities. She did not think faith was just about what you believed, it was also about how you behaved. "Religion must be *life made true*," she wrote. That's why she thought Christians should apply their faith to the pressing issues of the day, such as racism and poverty.

As a Black person who had achieved a level of professional success and education, Anna Julia Cooper saw it as her Christian duty to help others of her race who had not gained such advantages. She wrote, "Better to light a candle than curse the darkness. It has been my aim and hope to light candles that may carry on lighting others in God's own way of goodwill and helpful living."

From getting her PhD to writing history-making books to demanding excellence from all of her students, Cooper showed just how much Black people could learn and achieve when they had the opportunity. She did all of this in the Jim Crow era when laws made it almost impossible for Black people to get ahead. Anna Julia Cooper tapped into the spirit of justice to make sure that her people got the best education possible.

CHARLES HAMILTON HOUSTON

1895–1950

The Jim Crow era was a time of extreme racial segregation, but one case was about to change all that: *Brown v. Board of Education,* where the Supreme Court of the United States—the highest court in the land—finally declared that segregated education in public schools was unconstitutional. Even though most people have forgotten his name by now, the man who created the plan to end Jim Crow through the courts was a lawyer named Charles Hamilton Houston.

Compared to a lot of other Black people in his time, Charles H. Houston enjoyed a comfortable upbringing. As the only child of a successful Black lawyer and an attentive mother in Washington, D.C., his family's social and financial background helped give Houston a sense of safety and allowed him the freedom to study hard and excel in school. Houston graduated from Amherst College as a top student in his class. Then he joined the US Army, where he was commissioned as a second lieutenant and served in France and Germany during World War I. His experience in the army, however, exposed him to racism and discrimination from white soldiers. The experience was so painful that Houston later reflected, "I made up my mind that I would never get caught again without knowing something about my rights, and . . . I would study law and use my time fighting for men who couldn't strike back." That's what drove Houston to begin a remarkable career as a law student.

After his time in the army, Houston enrolled in Harvard Law School, where became the first Black person to serve on the editorial board of the *Harvard Law Review*. After graduation, he taught at Howard Law School, a historically Black college, and transformed it from a part-time, unaccredited night school into a highly respected institution accredited by the American Bar Association. Houston's leadership helped make Howard the destination school for Black lawyers. At one point, Howard Law trained approximately 25 percent of all Black lawyers in the country. Houston crafted his classroom on the basis that lawyers should be "social engineers." They had to use the law to shape a better society, and not just for personal gain. Nothing less than the best-prepared Black lawyers could engage in this struggle.

Houston's success at Howard Law gained the attention of the National Association for the Advancement of Colored People (NAACP), one of the largest and most well-known Black organizations of the time. He served as Special Counsel, or lawyer, for the organization and pioneered a new strategy to attack segregation. In a US Supreme Court case, he argued that the state of Missouri could not keep Black students from entering the state university law school because no "separate but equal" law school existed for Black students. The goal of the lawsuit was to use racists' own words against them. If the white establishment wanted to have separate facilities for Black and white people, then they must make them equal, as the *Plessy v. Ferguson*—the 1896 court case that established racial segregation as legal—stated. But Houston knew this would be far too hard for states to do.

His argument was successful. Houston trained and mentored many students, including Thurgood Marshall, who would later serve as the first Black justice on the US Supreme Court. In 1954, a challenge to legalized segregation finally made it to the highest court in the land with the *Brown v. Board of Education* case. Thurgood Marshall presented the argument against segregation, and he used the everything he had learned from his mentor Charles Hamilton Houston to make his case. He said that "separate but equal" was impossible to practice in the real world. It would mean two bus systems, two school systems, two hospital systems, two of everything—one for Black people and one for white people. No state or country had the money to keep life separate and truly equal based on race. His argument worked. The *Brown v. Board of Education* decision overturned legalized segregation and signaled the beginning of the end of the Jim Crow era.

Even though Houston and his team won many cases and opened new ways to fight for Black civil rights in the courts, Hamilton paid a price for working so much and so hard. He divorced his first wife, and when he remarried, he had little time for his second wife and son. Houston had also been sick for a long time, and his obsession with work only made it worse. He died of heart failure at the age of fifty-four.

Throughout his career, Houston held on to a strong Christian faith. His father, William, was the son of a pastor and it instilled in him a sharp sense of duty. His mother had a deep and devout faith that she used to lead her son Charles to develop a "keen religious-moral sense." Houston was such a dedicated Christian that he sometimes criticized the church for not standing up for justice enough. In a speech he gave in 1934, Hamilton told his audience, "The trouble is that most of our churches are social clubs masquerading under the guise of religious institutions." But the hypocrisy of some Christians could not make Hamilton give up on his faith.

Houston's dedication to Black progress helped him build both Howard Law School and the NAACP into long-lasting institutions that led to Black progress. He knew that changed laws could make life better not just for a few people, but for the whole country. Houston's life and work are an example of how the spirit of justice showed up in the law, the courts, and the legal profession to make the nation better.

The
CIVIL RIGHTS ERA
Late 1940s–Late 1960s

Medgar Evers, the husband of Myrlie Evers, was a military veteran. During World War II, he fought with the US Army and saw combat in France and Germany. He risked his life defending the values of freedom and democracy that the United States was supposed to represent. During the war, he'd also received military training and gained a broader perspective from seeing different parts of the world—as a result, he and other Black veterans were ready to be included as full citizens in their home country.

But when Evers returned to the US, he faced more battles. On July 2, 1946 (his twenty-first birthday), he celebrated by leading a group of fellow veterans to the courthouse in Decatur, Mississippi. They wanted to register to vote—their most basic political right as citizens. When they arrived, a group of white men armed with guns forced them to turn away. Even as soldiers who had served their country, Black people were still treated like second-class citizens. Though this treatment did not scare Medgar Evers. Instead, it emboldened Evers and people like him to take even greater risks for the sake of freedom.

Through the decades of the Jim Crow era, Black people and their allies never stopped resisting racism. Through all the lynchings, segregation, and insults, they kept building institutions, praying, and hoping for a better day. After many long years, all their work came bursting onto newspaper headlines and TV cameras around the country with marches, boycotts, speeches, and thousands of people working together for change. This era of activism was called the civil rights movement.

The fight for civil rights happened in many ways. Some people fought to change laws through the courts. For instance, a nine-year-old girl named Linda Brown became part of history when the Supreme Court took up her case. Linda couldn't go to the school that was closest to her house because it was for white kids only. She and her family joined with other Black families in a case called *Brown v. Board of Education*—the case that brought legal racial segregation tumbling down. Civil rights activists also took to the streets. In Birmingham in 1963, for instance, young people in junior high and high school joined the adults in protesting for equality. They were met by white police officers spraying them with firehoses, bringing out police K9 dog units, and arresting them. Other civil rights work was less public but no less important. Thousands of people printed flyers to advertise upcoming events, prayed and sang for strength in churches, opened their homes to activists visiting from around the country, and more. The movement for civil rights needed all kinds of people doing a variety of activities.

The civil rights movement resulted in more gains for Black people and other victims of injustice. In 1964, President Lyndon B. Johnson signed the Civil Rights Act into law in response to pressure from activists. The act made it illegal to discriminate based on race, color, religion, national origin, or gender.

In 1965, the Voting Rights Act was signed into law. It made it harder to stop someone from voting just because of their race. It got rid of unfair practices such as literacy tests, where Black people had to answer questions about politics or the Constitution but white people got easier questions or didn't have to test at all. The Voting Rights Act provided a way for the federal government to check on certain areas to make sure they were not preventing Black people and others from voting. As a result, it led to large increases in Black voter registration for the first time in US history.

The 1968 Fair Housing Act helped Black people live in homes and neighborhoods that had been off-limits under segregation. The new law made racial discrimination illegal when it came to buying, selling, renting, or getting housing loans based on race, color, religion, gender, or nationality. It also gave Black people and others the ability to file a complaint with the federal government if they experienced discrimination.

Of course, racism never goes down without a fight. Throughout the civil rights movement, activists faced strong resistance from people who did not want the nation to change and treat Black people more fairly. On September 15, 1963, a white supremacist planted dynamite at the 16th Street Baptist Church and killed four Black girls—Addie Mae Collins (fourteen), Denise McNair (eleven), Carole Robertson (fourteen), and Cynthia Wesley (fourteen). It shocked and outraged the country, but the grief did not stop the attacks. Earlier that summer, Medgar Evers had been assassinated in Jackson, Mississippi. Just weeks before that, the campaign to desegregate local businesses in Birmingham, Alabama, resulted in law enforcement officers using fire hoses and police dogs against Black protesters, many of them children. In June 1963, a civil rights activist named Fannie Lou Hamer and her friends were severely beaten in a jail in Mississippi. The late 1960s saw uprisings in urban Black communities in protest of police brutality and horrible living conditions in segregated housing. Many Black people died in these uprisings because law enforcement used lethal methods to stop them. Then in 1968, the most well-known leader of the civil rights movement, Martin Luther King Jr., was assassinated in Memphis by a white supremacist. The King had died.

But the dream of freedom and equality lived on. The civil rights movement was more than a social justice movement—it was a spiritual one. Black people and their allies rallied at churches, sang gospel songs, and prayed before, during, and after marches. Black churches acted as home bases and rallying points for the movement. Many of the movement's most significant leaders—such as Coretta Scott King, Prathia Hall, and Anna Arnold Hedgeman—were all people of faith. They felt the spirit of justice well up within them, giving them strength to send the walls of segregation and Jim Crow crumbling down.

ELLA BAKER
1903–1986

Ella Baker was all about the people. Even though journalists and others loved to focus on the larger-than-life leaders of the civil rights movement, Baker believed that real power—and the real work of the movement— was with regular people. She famously said, "Strong people don't need strong leaders." By this she meant that if you train and support everyday folks, then they don't need a famous person to lead them; they can take ownership of their own future.

Baker was born on December 13, 1903, in Norfolk, Virginia. Her grandmother told her stories about the hardships she'd faced under slavery and also shared the strength and bravery that Black people showed under the worst conditions. Hearing these stories helped Baker develop a sense of justice from an early age. Her family also owned a farm, which was not common for Black families in those days, and that gave Baker a sense that Black people could provide for themselves when given the opportunity.

She went to Shaw University in North Carolina and graduated as valedictorian of her class. She then moved to New York City and quickly became involved in justice and activism. Baker was part of several organizations, including the Young Negroes Cooperative League, women's rights groups, and, starting in 1938, the National Association for the Advancement of Colored People (NAACP). With the NAACP, she played a central role as Director of Branches, helping start and support new branches of the NAACP in communities around the nation.

In 1958, Baker relocated to Atlanta, Georgia, so she could be part of the Southern Christian Leadership Conference (SCLC) headed by Martin Luther King Jr. She ran the SCLC's headquarters in Atlanta. When the SCLC's executive director resigned in 1959, Baker—with her leadership skills and experience—was a natural choice to replace him. But the organization only made her the temporary director and replaced her when a man was found to fill the role. "I had known, number one, that there would never be any role for me in the leadership capacity with SCLC. Why? First, I'm a woman. Also, I'm not a minister." Baker was disappointed but not surprised. Many Black women in the movement endured disrespect and sexism (discrimination against women).

The next year, in February 1960, Black college students in Greensboro, North Carolina, staged the first sit-ins of the civil rights movement. Four Black students from North Carolina A&T sat at the lunch counter at the Woolworth's store downtown and waited to be served. The workers at the segregated store asked them to leave because the counter was only for whites, but the students politely refused. The sit-in movement had begun and it spread quickly. They were called sit-ins because protesters went into segregated restaurants and businesses and actually sat down—they faced arrest and even physical injury because they refused to move until the business treated Black people equally. By the end of the month, more than fifty thousand students across the nation had participated in sit-ins.

The students knew they were on to something. Newspapers and television programs ran stories about the sit-ins, and business owners slowly began changing their policies so Black customers could eat and shop without any trouble. Soon the students started talking about forming an organization to continue their protest efforts. Ella Baker convinced Martin Luther King Jr. to host a conference for the students in North Carolina. King wanted the students to form an organization that would become the student division of the SCLC that he led. But Baker persuaded the students to think about forming their own organization. The result was the Student Nonviolent Coordinating Committee (SNCC). Baker was convinced that "the young people were the hope of any movement . . . They were the people who kept the spirit going." She wanted to see them lead themselves and follow their own beliefs about how to pursue justice.

Baker left the SCLC later in 1960 and devoted more of her time to serving as a mentor to the young students in SNCC, who usually called her Miss Baker because she was decades older than them. Like King, Baker was committed to nonviolent direct action in the form of protests and demonstrations. She helped SNCC students organize the Freedom Rides in 1961 that saw groups of Black and white people try to ride on public transportation to test desegregation laws. As the Freedom Riders traveled on buses through the South, people who were committed to segregation refused to let them use the bathroom at rest stops, did not serve them in restaurants, and even beat up the activists. In 1964, Ella Baker helped the students organize Freedom Summer in Mississippi to help Black people in one of the poorest and most racist states in the country. Student volunteers spent their summer break doing a variety of activities that included voter registration, education, food programs, and more. This was not an easy summer break. Students often risked arrest, beatings, or even murder for their actions.

Ella Baker died on December 13, 1986 (her birthday) at the age of eighty-three. Her ability to honor people just as they were came from her commitment to grassroots leadership. She saw how ego and pride could ruin the work of the civil rights movement, and she deeply believed that the people had the power. All they needed was the right opportunity to show it. Ella Baker dedicated her life to building up the spirit of justice in other people.

FANNIE LOU HAMER

1917–1977

Fannie Lou Hamer didn't want to go to church . . . at least not on a Monday night. But her friend convinced her to come along to William Chapel Missionary Baptist Church in Ruleville, Mississippi, and what she heard that night changed her life forever. She heard activists talk about civil rights and how it was important for Black people to vote in elections so they could choose their own leaders. When the presenters asked for volunteers to register to vote, Hamer said, "I raised my hand as high as it could go."

Hamer had little to gain and everything to lose by becoming active in the civil rights movement. She was the twentieth of twenty children born into a sharecropping family—imagine having nineteen brothers and sisters! She grew up very poor. Sometimes her family only had some greens without any seasoning and grease mixed with flour to eat. Hamer started picking cotton at the age of six, when the owner of the plantation where her family lived promised her candy if she could pick fifty pounds of cotton that week. She never stopped picking cotton after that. In fact, she had to drop out of school in sixth grade so she could pick cotton full time. When she grew up, she married a share-cropper named Perry "Pap" Hamer, and they picked cotton too.

When Hamer went to register to vote, she and nearly twenty others were met by a group of white men holding guns. They were forced to give up and go home. When Hamer got back to the plantation where she worked and lived, the white plantation owner, W.D. Marlow, fired Hamer and kicked her off the plantation for just attempting to register to vote.

Losing her home and job only motivated Hamer. She said, "They kicked me off the plantation, they set me free. It's the best thing that could happen. Now I can work for my people." And work she did. Hamer became an outspoken civil rights activist. She joined the Student Nonviolent Coordinating Committee, a group of young people who were often viewed as radicals because they were almost fearless in confronting racism in the segregated South. But then tragedy struck.

In June 1963, Fannie Lou Hamer was coming back from some civil rights training on a bus with other activists. They stopped at a bus terminal and restaurant in a tiny town called Winona, Mississippi. The white café workers and customers did not want any Black people there, and the police got involved. They arrested Hamer and several of her friends and took them all to jail. Then they took them one by one into a cell and hit them with blackjacks—wooden sticks covered with leather. Hamer barely survived the beating, and she said her body felt swollen and "hard as bone." For the rest of her life, she had kidney damage and a permanent limp. But if the police officers thought they had scared Hamer, they were wrong. She went right back to work for civil rights.

In 1964, Fannie Lou Hamer had the important opportunity to share her story in front of the Democratic National Convention, where people in the Democratic party gathered to select their candidates for election. In Mississippi, racist white people kept Black people from voting and from serving as delegates—official representatives of the state—during national conventions. Hamer and others from the newly formed Mississippi Freedom Democratic Party were there to insist on Black participation. The group selected Hamer as one of their speakers. She gave a dramatic testimony of the violence and opposition she faced trying to vote in Mississippi, and she included the horrible story of her torture in a Mississippi jail. She ended by asking, "Is this America, the land of the free and the home of the brave, where we [are] threatened daily, because we want to live as decent human beings, in America?" Her ability to speak plainly and boldly made that speech the most memorable part of the convention.

Hamer kept fighting for civil rights, and she also worked to help the poor. She started the Freedom Farm Cooperative and got some land so she and others could raise their own food instead of depending on someone else. She also started a "pig bank." A poor family got a pregnant pig, and when it gave birth, they would give some of the piglets back to the farm and keep some for themselves so everyone could have a chance to have their own meat. In spite of all her bravery, Hamer died poor and nearly alone in 1977. Yet her life shines as an example for people today.

Hamer drew strength from her faith. Even with all the suffering she faced, her religion taught her to love others and hold out hope for change. "How can we say we love God and hate our brothers and sisters?" she asked. Through all her years of activism, she became well-known for her powerful singing voice, and she would often sing church songs. One of her favorites was "This Little Light of Mine." She would use her voice to encourage people and remind them of a power beyond themselves. Fannie Lou Hamer let her light shine.

MARTIN LUTHER KING JR.

1929–1968

The civil rights movement could not have happened without the participation of thousands and thousands of people. No single leader led the movement; it took a village. But the most famous and well-known leader of the movement is Martin Luther King Jr. Over time, though, King has become less of a man and more of a myth.

King was smart. He started college at fifteen through a special program happening during World War II. After graduating from Morehouse College, King went to Crozier Theological Seminary in Pennsylvania, his first time living outside the South. After that, he went to Boston University for his PhD in theology. While in Boston he met Coretta Scott, whom he married. King loved to study and learn. He thought he'd become a professor, but life had other plans.

His father was a preacher at Ebenezer Baptist Church in Atlanta, which King called his "second home." In 1948, when King was just nineteen, his father ordained him to preach. After he finished his PhD, he became pastor of Dexter Avenue Baptist Church in Montgomery, Alabama. In 1955, the Montgomery Improvement Association held a meeting at the church about a potential bus boycott, and they chose King as a spokesperson. From his first speech, it was clear he was an inspirational speaker, and he became the movement's public leader.

Civil rights activists organized the March on Washington for Jobs and Freedom to push lawmakers in the nation's capital to write laws that would help Black people and poor people. They demanded changes such as a program to give all adults jobs, a national minimum wage so workers had enough money for food and housing, and penalties for businesses or states that refused to treat people equally. The crowd on the day of the march—August 28, 1963—was huge: 250,000 people from all over the country showed up. They held up signs that said "Freedom Now" and they sang songs like "We Shall Overcome." At the end of the march, people gathered in front of the Lincoln Memorial in Washington, D.C., to hear from musicians and actors and listen to speeches from organizers and politicians. Here, Martin Luther King Jr. delivered his most well-known words in the "I Have a Dream" speech.

Those working for civil rights faced violence from racist community members and even law enforcement officials. But what made the movement so remarkable and effective is that the protesters were mostly nonviolent. King was inspired by Mahatma Gandhi and the nonviolent movement he led in India. In fact, King and his wife, Coretta, traveled to India for a month in 1959, and he came back saying, "Since being in India, I am more convinced than ever before that the method of nonviolent resistance is the most potent weapon available to oppressed people in their struggle for justice and human dignity." King committed himself to confronting the violence and hate of racism with the love and patience of nonviolence. For King, being nonviolent did not mean running away. It was just the opposite. He and other nonviolent resisters put themselves in the way of danger on purpose to demonstrate the righteousness of their cause and reveal the brutality of racism.

Even though we now celebrate King with a holiday and we frequently share his words, he was not very popular while he was alive. In 1966, 63 percent of people had an unfavorable view of King. Fifty percent thought he was doing more to hurt the civil rights movement than help it. In 1968, King was shot and killed at a motel in Memphis, Tennessee. Even after his death, 31 percent of people thought he had brought it on himself. Part of the reason many did not like King was his views on issues other than racism. Toward the end of his life, King talked about the "three evils"—poverty, racism, and militarism. He did not like the use of violence in any form, including in wars. When he spoke out against the Vietnam War, many of his former supporters turned against him because they thought he was unpatriotic. King also had much to say about poverty. He could not be at peace with the United States, where some people had more money and food than they needed while so many others could hardly eat or didn't have a place to live. When King said that we as a society would have to share our money with the poor, he became even more unpopular.

King's lifetime of sacrifice, leadership, and courage make him the most famous representative of the spirit of justice during the civil rights movement. His faith sustained him through the death threats and pressure of helping to lead the movement. In a moment when he felt like giving up, he heard an inner voice from God saying, "Martin Luther, stand up for righteousness. Stand up for justice. Stand up for truth. And lo I will be with you, even until the end of the world.' . . . I heard the voice of Jesus saying still to fight on." In that moment, he knew God would be with him no matter what happened.

Over time, the human being has been somewhat overshadowed by the legend that arose after his murder. Today, most people remember King for just one of his speeches, but they don't read the thousands of words he wrote in his books. They remember him for being nonviolent, but they don't recall his thoughts on jobs and economics. They remember him as a leader, but they don't see him as a husband and a father. They remember him marching in the streets, but don't remember his preaching in the pulpit. They remember him for a holiday in his honor, but they forget how much he was dishonored while he was alive. It is good to remember all that King accomplished and what he stood for, but we need to study King's life more closely so we have a better knowledge of the real person behind the history.

CORETTA SCOTT KING
1927–2006

Coretta Scott King begins her autobiography with the words, "There is a Mrs. King. There is also Coretta. How one became detached from the other remains a mystery to me." Coretta Scott King was a mother and the wife of Martin Luther King Jr., but she was also a global human rights activist who worked her entire life to make life better for others. She should be remembered not just for who her husband was but for who she was too.

Corretta Scott was born on April 27, 1927, in Heiberger, Alabama. She was one of three children and grew up on the farm her family owned. She milked cows, raised crops, and tended to the livestock. Both Scott and her parents had deep faith in God. Even after white people in the community burned down their family's home, her father led them in prayer and told them to forgive the culprits. She grew up attending Tabor AME Zion Church, and she and her family would walk the four miles to and from church each week. At the age of ten, Coretta made a profession of faith and joined the church.

Coretta's mother instilled in her daughter the dream of an education, something that was rare for young women, especially Black women, in those days. During high school, Scott attended Lincoln Normal School, where she graduated as valedictorian of her class.

In high school, she studied classical music and the work of legendary Black musical talents such as Paul Robeson and Marian Anderson, and she dreamed of being a famous concert singer. Scott also learned about pacifism and first encountered Bayard Rustin, a nonviolent protester and activist who would later be a key organizer of the March on Washington for Jobs and Freedom in 1963. Scott recalled being "fascinated by Rustin's lecture on how conflict could be resolved without war or bloodshed." Long before meeting Martin Luther King Jr., Coretta Scott had already begun thinking about nonviolent protest and how to use it in the movement for Black freedom.

After graduating, Scott attended Antioch College in Ohio. In a time when Black and white students often could not go to school together, Scott said that Antioch was a "pioneer in multicultural living and education." She had two white roommates and, for the first time, began understanding white people beyond the racism she had experienced. She also was exposed to other religions, such as Islam and Buddhism. She became involved with the local NAACP chapter and learned more about the philosophy of nonviolence. "I began to consider myself a pacifist. Pacifism felt right to me; it accorded with what I had been taught as a Christian: to love thy neighbor as thyself." Her experiences in school and her increasing commitment to peace activism gave Scott a vision of what would later be called the "Beloved Community." The Beloved Community described a new nation and world that treated people with dignity and respect—where wars had ended and everyone had what they needed for life, liberty, and happiness.

After her time at Antioch College, the talented Scott applied to some of the nation's best musical schools. She gained an invitation to study at the New England Conservatory of Music in Boston, and it was during her time there she met Martin Luther King Jr. Although she wasn't impressed with him at first, she began to like him and saw how their visions for Black uplift could be a good match. They were married in 1953, and she was by his side during his work as the most prominent leader of the civil rights movement. Their marriage was cut violently short by an assassin's bullet while Martin Luther King Jr. stood on the balcony of the Lorraine Motel in Memphis, Tennessee. Coretta Scott King had to find a way to both grieve her husband's murder and carry on the work of the movement at the same time.

After her husband's assassination, Coretta Scott King made preserving his memory a part of her mission. Even with the heartbreak and relentless demands of being a newly single parent, Scott King continued to work. She often called the King Center for Nonviolent Social Change in Atlanta her "fifth child." She founded the center on June 26, 1968, just over two months after her husband's assassination. As its leader, she dedicated the center to continuing the tradition of nonviolent social change and love in action. The center allowed Scott King to not only commemorate her husband's life but also refine her own ideas about the work that still needed to be done for civil rights.

After her husband's assassination, Coretta Scott King led the effort to make Martin Luther King Jr. Day a national holiday. It took fifteen years, but in 1983 the King's birthday became a national day off to remember his life and the movement for Black civil rights. Scott King expanded her focus on racial justice to include the global struggle for equality. In particular, she became an outspoken activist against apartheid, a system of segregation in South Africa. In 1986, she took part in an important trip to South Africa, where she met with prominent African leaders and promoted the end of apartheid.

Coretta Scott King was an activist before she met MLK Jr., and she was an activist after his murder. She poured her life out serving all kinds of marginalized groups of people around the world, focusing not only on racial justice but also women's rights, the end of apartheid, nuclear disarmament, and LGBTQ rights. Throughout her many campaigns and initiatives to bring about the Beloved Community and promote nonviolence, her faith always guided her. In times of fear, grief, and uncertainty, Coretta Scott King consistently relied on her belief in God and hope for progress to guide her.

ANNA ARNOLD HEDGEMAN

1899–1990

Even in her teenage years, Anna Arnold Hedgeman believed in Jesus as the "tough courageous Son of God who studied, worked, dreamed, planned, and lived to produce change in his turbulent world." She did not believe in a "by and by" faith that was only concerned about the afterlife, but a "here and now" faith that got involved in the real lives of people as they existed in the present. It was that faith and the commitment to serve others that led Hedgeman to become a teacher, an administrator with the Young Women's Christian Association (YWCA), and one of the only women involved with the planning of the March on Washington in 1963.

Hedgeman was born on July 5, 1899, just one day after the Fourth of July and a few months before the dawn of a new century. There weren't many Black people where she grew up in Anoka, Minnesota. Her father had moved there from South Carolina in search of more freedom and opportunities. Although he was Black, people often assumed he was white because of his light skin.

Anna Arnold Hedgeman grew up in the church. Her father made sure that Christianity was central in his family's life. He led the family in prayer twice a day. Every week, they would have Sunday "program" where her father expected the children to review that week's sermon and Sunday school lesson. As she later recalled of her childhood, "One lived to work, plan, study, discipline one's self, search for truth, and pray for God's guidance." Her faith was such an important part of her life that when Hedgeman went off to college, she attended a school that was connected to the Methodist church, Hamline University. She also became the first Black graduate in the school's history.

After college, she couldn't get a teaching job in Minnesota, so Hedgeman traveled far from home both in terms of distance and culture. Even just getting to Mississippi became an experience of racism when the Black train attendant explained segregated transportation to her and pointed her out of the "white" car and back to the "colored" car. When she finally arrived in Mississippi, she couldn't even get a taxi because no white driver would allow a Black woman in their vehicle. She taught college for a brief time and saw firsthand how vicious racism could be. Her students struggled with college because their segregated and unequal schools had not equipped them well for higher education. After just two years, Hedgeman left Mississippi, but the hardships she saw and experienced there gave her a lifelong passion for racial justice.

After trying out a few different jobs, Hedgeman ended up at the National Council of Churches, which brought all kinds of churches together into a support network. In 1963, at the height of the civil rights movement, they formed the Commission on Race and Religion (CRR). The commissioner's leader brought on Anna Arnold Hedgeman, who was by then in her sixties, to help with the CRR's mission.

In her work with the CRR, Hedgeman helped with some of the planning for the March on Washington in 1963. She served on the powerful administrative committee that was pulling the whole event together. On a flyer advertising the march, she was the only woman listed as an organizer. Hedgeman was an excellent bridge builder—her role was bringing together leaders of different civil rights organizations, who loved to argue with each other, so they could plan one of the largest protest demonstrations in US history. Hedgeman used her connections and resourcefulness to get women's groups to support the march. In most churches and civil rights organizations, the women outnumber the men and do much of the work, so the march could not have happened without the support of these women's groups. Hedgeman also used her experiences with white people while growing up in Minnesota to help recruit more than 40,000 white Christians to attend the march. In total, 250,000 demonstrators marched on Washington, D.C., for greater economic and civil rights. That success is owed in part to the work of Anna Arnold Hedgeman.

A few weeks after the march, disaster struck the movement for civil rights. On September 15, 1963, four girls were killed in a racial terrorist attack when a bomb exploded at the 16th Street Baptist Church in Birmingham, Alabama. The tragedy challenged Hedgeman's faith as she wondered how people could be so hateful, they'd kill four children. But the attack only made her more determined to work for justice. She helped pull together Christians to support the Civil Rights Act of 1964, which included many actions to grant Black people more rights. When the president finally signed the bill into law, Hedgeman was among guests that attended a special ceremony at the White House.

Hedgeman went from a very religious and small world in Minnesota to the Jim Crow South of Mississippi, and on to significant work with the Council on Race and Religion. She labored to bring people of faith together to fight racism and to follow the spirit of justice.

PRATHIA HALL

1940–2002

There might not have been an "I Have a Dream" speech if it hadn't been for a Black woman named Prathia Hall. Many sources credit her with using the phrase "I have a dream" long before King's speech at the March on Washington in 1963. But her life and work go far beyond one simple saying.

Prathia Hall was born in Philadelphia in 1940. Like many other activists, she grew up as a preacher's kid. Her father not only was a pastor, he also started a church—Mt. Sharon Baptist Church—in 1938. Hall and her siblings practically lived at the church since they participated in all its activities, like helping with the food pantry and visiting sick people who couldn't leave their homes.

Hall's religious beliefs also shaped her views on racism. She felt that "God intends us to be free, and assists us, and empowers us in the struggle for freedom." She called this way of viewing religion and activism "freedom faith," and she practiced it from a very early age. "Well it sounds presumptuous to say you were born with a mission, but I have always had a deep passion for justice," she said.

In her teenage years and early twenties, Hall went to work for freedom. She attended talks and presentations by civil rights activists and learned all she could about the movement. In 1962, she quit college and joined the Student Nonviolent Coordinating Committee (SNCC) so she could take a more active role in the struggle for Black freedom.

It was during her time in SNCC that Hall used the "I have a dream" phrase. She was at a vigil to remember four Black churches that had recently been burned down by white supremacists. Organizers asked her to give the opening prayer. As she bowed her head, she asked God to bring about a better future. She said again and again, "I have a dream." Martin Luther King Jr. was in the audience that day and Hall's powerful prayer left an impression on him. After the service, King looked for Hall and asked for permission to use the phrase. Hall said yes, and King famously used it at the March on Washington. Now "I have a dream" is one of the most well-known parts of any speech ever given during the civil rights movement.

"I have a dream" was more than just an inspiring phrase. The word *dream* is a form of imagination. It is hard for an oppressed people to dream. They are too busy just figuring out how to survive—how to get a job, earn enough money to support themselves, and find their way in a culture that is against them because of their race or ethnicity. But when Prathia Hall spoke and prayed about a dream, she pictured a world where everyone had what they needed. No one struggled simply to survive; they could thrive, and play, and create as they were meant to do by God.

As skilled as Hall was in talking about religion, it was very uncommon at the time for women to be preachers. She wanted very much to be a pastor, but she knew "almost no ordained women ministers were taken seriously." However, her gifts could not be denied. Even Martin Luther King Jr. said, "Prathia Hall is the one platform speaker I would prefer not to follow." In 1977, the American Baptist Church ordained Hall as one of their very first women pastors. Her father had tragically died in a trolley accident, which not only devastated his family but meant the church he founded need a pastor. Hall was able to step in and pastor the church her father started.

Hall continued to practice "freedom faith" for the rest of her life. After the civil rights movement, she went back to school and earned several degrees in theology—the study of God. She became a well-respected college professor and preacher. Through her research, teaching, and writing, Prathia Hall helped spread "womanist" ideas. Womanism explains and applies biblical truths with a specific focus on Black women. She wanted people to be free of prejudice whether it was based on race, gender, or both.

Hall's "freedom faith" could also be called the spirit of justice. Her work with the Student Nonviolent Coordinating Committee and her determination to be a pastor at a time when most places would not accept women in the role demonstrates how the spirit of justice worked itself out in her life. She understood that religion did not begin or end in the walls of a church building. Faith had to be lived. It had to take risks, face danger, and hold on to the dream of a better tomorrow. Prathia Hall had a freedom faith and a dream.

UNITA BLACKWELL

1933–2019

Unita Blackwell had to have some kind of imagination to come up with the idea of being mayor of a town in Mississippi. Although she worked hard and was intelligent, it was very unlikely that someone in her situation would become an elected official—in fact, it had never happened before in her state. But Blackwell did not mind a challenge and she had the determination to achieve whatever she set her mind to.

Unita (U-NEE-tuh) Blackwell was born in 1933 during the Great Depression. Lots of people were unemployed and struggling to get enough food to eat. Blackwell's family had it even harder because they were sharecroppers in the South, where folks had even less money. But she survived. Life was still hard, though. She only stayed in school through eighth grade because she had to quit and start working full time. She was in her thirties before she even knew she could vote, let alone run for an office like mayor of a town.

Blackwell's mother faithfully attended church. Church was the center of Black life in those days. "Church was the only place we could go that was not controlled by white people, and it completed our needs in every part of our lives. The church was our anchor. It held us together. It kept us going," Blackwell later explained. She spent countless hours in the church each week. At church, Blackwell learned about the Golden Rule—treat others the way you want to be treated—and tried to live her life that way, even when it came to white people. She had plenty of reasons to be upset about the racist society she lived in. A white man had shot and killed her grandfather years before. She faced discrimination of all kinds just because she was a Black woman. But she learned from the church that she should not hate. "Without my church and my faith that God would pull me through, I don't think I could have survived those days or been prepared to face the future." Those lessons helped her become a civil rights activist too.

In 1964, two Student Nonviolent Coordinating Committee (SNCC) members came to visit her church. They had arrived to tell Black people in Mississippi how to register to vote. Blackwell had just taught a Sunday school lesson with the topic "God helps those who help themselves," and one of the SNCC members repeated the phrase when he got up to talk. He said Black people had to help themselves by registering and then voting. When the organizers asked for volunteers, Blackwell stood up. Years later she said, "I've been standing up ever since."

Blackwell became a tireless and effective civil rights activist. She entered an election in her town, Mayersville, in 1976 and won, becoming the first Black woman to be mayor of any town in Mississippi. As mayor, Blackwell had her work cut out for her. The town only had about five hundred people, and it did not have indoor plumbing, some of the roads were not paved, and many of the houses were falling apart. Blackwell worked with state and federal government departments to get more money to fix up her town. She even worked to bring Black and white people together as she formed an interracial council to help support her efforts. Blackwell was such a good mayor that the town kept electing her, and she stayed in office until 2001.

Blackwell had come a long way from her childhood, with its poverty and lack of education. She had overcome the prejudices people had against Black people and women to become the mayor of her town. Everything changed for her once she got involved in civil rights work. "I was stuck in poverty and trapped by the color of my skin in a pointless existence. Then the movement came along and my mind opened up . . . my life had meaning." For many people, especially Black women, following the spirit of justice led them to a community, helped them develop skills, and gave them the confidence to achieve their highest potential.

DOROTHY HEIGHT

1912–2010

Most people look at the 1963 March on Washington as the most important moment of the civil rights movement, but one small meeting that happened right after might have been just as important. The very next day, Dorothy Height, who's often called the "Godmother of the Civil Rights Movement," set up a meeting of Black women. The theme was "After the March . . . What?" The purpose was to figure out how to make sure the march led to real changes for Black people. But an equally urgent task was to talk about the role of Black women and children in the movement.

These Black women were rightfully upset that none of the speakers at the march were Black women. Mahalia Jackson, a renowned gospel singer, sang a song and women were acknowledged, but none served as a main speaker. Sidelining women was an insult since Black women did so much of the planning, recruiting, organizing, and executing of the march. Dorothy Height was one of the most important people who worked on the march. She, along with Anna Arnold Hedgeman, had input in planning, and Height was the only woman who represented an actual women's organization involved in the effort. Still, even after the march, the sad tradition of putting women in the back of the civil rights bus, so to speak, continued. For the women at the "After the March . . . What?" meeting, the march only strengthened their conviction that they had to raise the concerns of Black women and families in the movement.

Dorothy Height was an ideal person to make sure those questions were heard. She was born in 1912 in Richmond, Virginia. When she was still a child, her family moved to a town near Pittsburgh, Pennsylvania. From her earliest days, her parents made a big deal about education, and she took their words seriously. She attended a racially integrated high school, and even as a teenager she began working for racial justice by supporting voting rights and anti-lynching campaigns. Her academic achievements earned her a full scholarship to attend the well-respected Barnard College in New York City. But the college said it already had all the Black students it was going to accept that year and so she could not attend. Height did not let this rejection stop her. She enrolled in New York University and earned not one but two degrees there—a bachelor's and master's degree.

Height had grown up next door to a church, Emmanuel Baptist Church, and she and her family were members there. Her family would often spend all of Sunday in church. Always a problem solver, Height noticed that the white children at the segregated Rankin Christian Center were often noisy and disruptive. Height came up with a plan to watch the kids and give them educational activities to keep them busy. The center's director agreed to her proposal and let Height teach Bible lessons to the children. Height was only twelve years old at the time.

In 1937, Height took a job with the Young Women's Christian Association (YWCA). In her work with the YWCA, she was a key figure in their attempts to desegregate in the middle of the 1900s. That is also the job where she met her mentor and inspiration, Mary Mcleod Bethune, a remarkable organizer and leader. Height helped the YWCA create a document called "The Interracial Charter and Related Policy." In it she wrote, "Wherever there is injustice on the basis of race, whether in the community, the nation or the world, our protest must be clear and our labor for its removal, vigorous and steady." She also helped create a permanent Office of Racial Justice at the YWCA and served as its first director. She retired in 1977 after forty years of service, and the organization honored her with a lifetime honorary status as a member of their leadership board.

At the same time she was working at the YWCA, Height also took a position as the fourth president of the National Negro Council of Women (NCNW). The NCNW was founded by Mary Mcleod Bethune, but she retired and two presidents followed her. Then Height took over and made the NCNW a critical organization during the civil rights movement. She was a champion of Black women's rights. This was a necessary focus because even women's groups led by white women did not make addressing racism or the particular issues Black women faced one of their priorities. Height later reflected, "It took a while for women's movement leaders to understand that some of the issues in which they were more focused had less appeal to black women . . ." Height was one of the most important leaders who paid attention to both Black civil rights and women's rights.

Dorothy Height continued working until she was ninety-eight years old. She never married or had children, and she focused her energy almost entirely on promoting racial justice and women's rights. Her decades of service earned her the Congressional Gold Medal and the Presidential Medal of Freedom, the country's highest honor given to a civilian. At her funeral in 2010, President Barack Obama said, "We remember her for all she did over a lifetime, behind the scenes, to broaden the movement's reach . . . To make us see the drive for civil rights and women's rights not as a separate struggle, but as part of a larger movement to secure the rights of all humanity."

The **LATE TWENTIETH CENTURY**

Early 1970s–1999

Stokely Carmichael had enough. On a humid Mississippi night in June 1966, the activist and leader from the Student Nonviolent Coordinating Committee (SNCC) hopped onto the back of a pickup truck and addressed the crowd standing in the field before him. "This is the twenty-seventh time I've been arrested. I ain't going to jail no more!" Carmichael was helping lead the March Against Fear that James Meredith—the first Black person to enroll at the University of Mississippi—had started a few days before. Meredith had been shot by a white supremacist on the second day of his solo march. He survived, but civil rights groups from around the country now joined his march from Memphis, Tennessee, to Jackson, Mississippi.

Stokely Carmichael was a young man originally from Trinidad who had joined the struggle for civil rights during the sit-ins started by Black college students. Now as a bold and experienced grassroots organizer (someone who works with ordinary people to chase a common goal), he had become frustrated with the slow pace of change. He thought the marches and singing used during the civil rights movement weren't working. He and other Black people wanted to take a different approach. "We been saying 'freedom' for six years and we ain't got nothin'. What we got to start saying now is 'black power'! We want black power! We want black power!" Carmichael was not the first person to use the phrase "black power," but this time it caught on. It would come to describe the next phase of the movement for racial justice.

While the civil rights movement and organizations such as the NAACP and the Southern Christian Leadership Conference led by Martin Luther King Jr. had brought attention to the terrible reality of segregation in the South, many Black people—especially in big northern cities—still felt frustrated. They were crammed into tiny, broken-down apartments and neighborhoods. Their schools had leaky roofs and books that were falling apart. The police roamed their neighborhoods and seemed to make up reasons to harass, beat, and even kill local residents. These communities wanted Black people to take control of their own situation and not wait for white people to agree with them.

In Oakland in 1966, two Black men—Huey P. Newton and Bobby Seale—formed the Black Panther Party for Self-Defense. They created the group with a focus on preventing police brutality in urban Black communities. They donned black berets and leather jackets and armed themselves with pistols, rifles, and other firearms. They set up patrols to follow police officers and monitor their interactions with community members. They put together a ten-point program that included demands such as: "We want freedom. We want power to determine the destiny of our Black Community," "We want an immediate end to POLICE BRUTALITY and MURDER of Black people," and "We want education that teaches us our true history and our role in present-day society."

This frustration boiled over into destructive and deadly uprisings in cities such as Los Angeles, Detroit, and Newark, New Jersey. In response to this string of events, President Lyndon B. Johnson created the National Advisory Commission on Civil Disorders, otherwise known as the "Kerner Commission" because of its chairperson, Governor Otto Kerner of Illinois. The commission answered three questions: What happened? Why did it happen? And what can prevent it from happening again? After seven months of site visits, interviews, and research, the committee released its findings in February 1968. The report stated, "Our Nation is moving toward two societies, one black, one white— separate and unequal." The commissioners pointed out a fact that many did not want to hear. "What white Americans have never fully understood but what the Negro can never forget—is that white society is deeply implicated in the ghetto. White institutions created it, white institutions maintain it, and white society condones it."

The late twentieth century, from the early 1970s to the end of the 1990s, saw the United States struggling to figure out what would come next after Jim Crow and legal segregation. Almost overnight, it seemed like the country had changed and racism was no longer acceptable to most people. But overall opinions don't change very quickly, and laws and organizations change even more slowly. People who feared racial progress organized themselves to oppose any more shifts in society.

In 1979, a white Christian minister named Jerry Falwell started an organization called the Moral Majority. Their program was simple: "Get 'em saved, get 'em baptized, and get 'em registered [to vote]." But the Moral Majority was not simply about getting people to know Jesus and participate in elections. It had a specific set of ideas it wanted to spread. People leading the Moral Majority thought that the United States had lost its way, and that the movement for civil rights was a large part of the problem. They believed that political conservativism was the answer. The Moral Majority gathered Christians to support Republican politicians such as Ronald Reagan for president. Over time, groups like the Moral Majority and others encouraged their followers to think that the only "Christian" way to vote was Republican, and that policies meant to help Black people, women, the poor, and others were bad for America. This movement came to be called the "Religious Right" and it emerged, in part, because of the racial progress of the 1960s.

Even with increasing opposition during the period from 1970s to the 1990s, Black people and a growing number of people from many other groups resisted efforts to roll back civil rights and continued to pull the nation forward into a better future. New leaders arose such as James Cone, Shirley Chisholm, and Sister Thea Bowman. They found the spirit of justice in the days after the civil rights movement and struggled against the racial prejudice that still sank into the systems of society.

JAMES CONE
1938–2018

Is God real? What is God like? What does "honor thy father and mother" mean in the Ten Commandments? How do I get to heaven?

If you've ever asked questions like these or had any other questions about God, spirituality, and holiness, then you are asking questions of theology. Theology is the study of God. For a long time, the kind of theology taught in schools and written about in books came mostly from Europeans and white people. People all over the world and from every tribe and nation did theology, but their beliefs weren't as well-known. James Cone helped change that.

James Cone is often called "the Founder of Black Liberation Theology." *Liberation* means "freedom," and Cone helped spread a theology of Black freedom. During the 1960s and 1970s, Cone was paying attention to the events of the civil rights and Black Power movements. In 1967, Black people in Detroit revolted against police brutality in what became the deadliest urban rebellion at that time. Cone was filled with anger at how Black people were being treated, and he wrote, "My explosion shook me at the core of my racial identity, killing the 'Negro' in me and resurrecting my black self." What died in Cone was a spirit of fear and powerlessness, and what came alive in him was the spirit of justice to fight oppression through theology.

James Cone was born in Arkansas in 1938. He grew up in the segregated conditions of the Jim Crow South and personally knew the white-fisted grip that racism could hold over entire communities. He attended Philander Smith College, a historically Black college (HBCU) in Little Rock, and was in the city during a historic showdown in 1957. Arkansas's governor, Orval Faubus, disobeyed the law and ordered National Guard troops to block nine Black students from entering Central High School. The president himself had to get involved and send in the US Army just to make sure the Black students could attend classes with white students. Cone continued his education at Garrett Theological Seminary near Chicago and got a PhD in systematic theology at a time when very few Black people held that degree. He taught theology at a few places until he ended up at Union Theological Seminary in New York City, where he spent the rest of his career and built his legacy as an influential theological thinker.

Until about 1966, most civil rights protesters used the slogan *Freedom Now*. You can see this phrase written on posters at the March on Washington and many other protests as well. But during the mid-1960s and 1970s, the phrase *Black power* became more common. James Cone started using this language because it represented strength, independence, and confrontation for Black people who were frustrated that change for Black people was not coming fast enough. To James Cone, Black power was the key idea missing from European and white theology.

Cone published his most well-known book, *Black Theology and Black Power*, in 1969. Black Liberation Theology, as his teachings were called, put the Black experience at the center of understanding God and the Bible. Black experiences of slavery, segregation, racism, and injustice shaped how Cone thought and taught about faith.

In his book, he wrote a phrase that was controversial to some and celebrated by others: "Jesus is black." Cone explained that Jesus is Black because Jesus always identified with the weakest, most oppressed, and most rejected people in society. In Jesus's earthly life, those people were often the Jews, who were under the control of the Roman empire. Jesus himself was a Jew, which meant—according to Cone—that he identified with the poor and the powerless in all times and places. "To say that Christ is black means that black people are God's poor people whom Christ has come to liberate," he wrote. It wasn't about his skin color—though Jesus was brown-skinned and not white like in many pictures that represent him. More important to Cone, Jesus was Black because he put himself on the side of the poor and downtrodden.

James Cone's version of Black Liberation Theology opened up a whole new field of questions and arguments in theological studies. His work inspired many others to begin speaking more boldly about God from their perspective as people who experienced injustice. Latin American, Asian, and women theologians worked hard to show how God related to them and their situations. In their work, Jesus would no longer be considered European or white. People would no longer accept the idea that Jesus was on the side of the rich and powerful, a group who often made life hard for others who weren't as fortunate. Instead, Jesus could be found with the large groups of people who did not have much money, weren't elected to a political office, and had nothing but their faith and courage to resist evil. Cone used his career as a scholar to be a "theological witness of the black freedom struggle" and helped spark a revolution in Christian theology in the United States.

SHIRLEY CHISHOLM

1924–2005

Shirley Chisholm would have been fantastic on social media. Her creative use of words would have gone viral. She had one of the most memorable political campaign slogans of the twentieth century— she was "Unbought and Unbossed." Chisholm ran for the US House of Representatives in 1968 and won. That made her the first Black woman in Congress. But she didn't stop there. She ran for president in 1972 and became the first Black woman to do so in one of the two major political parties. Throughout her entire political career, she could not be controlled by anyone, no matter how much money they had or how powerful they were. Even though her "Unbought and Unbossed" campaign slogan is memorable, it was her faith that made her powerful.

Chisholm was born in Brooklyn, New York, but she always considered her true home the island of Barbados. Her mother was from there, and after just a few years in the United States, she sent Shirley and her two siblings back to Barbados to live with their grandmother until she and her husband could save enough money to bring their children back to the US for school. Although Shirley's grandmother, Emily Seale, was strict, "there were endless hugs, laughter, tears, and chatter." Chisholm always remembered those brief years with her grandmother as a highlight in her life.

When she returned to her family in America, Sundays meant going back and forth to church three different times for various services. Chisholm's mother told her children, "You're going to grow up to be good Christians." Chisholm was an energetic child and didn't necessarily like going to church so much, but she had a respect for religion and took to heart the lessons she learned at church and from her mother.

Chisholm did well in high school, and when she graduated in 1942, she had college offers from Vassar and Oberlin College. But her parents could not afford to pay for room and board at these faraway schools, so she stayed closer to home and attended Brooklyn College. Nine out of ten students there were white, and Chisholm began to see how racism affected all of society. "Things were organized to keep those who were on top up there. The country was racist all the way through." But she worked hard and graduated with honors with a degree in education.

Chisholm worked for seven years as a teacher in Harlem while studying at night to earn a master's degree in education. She met a Jamaican immigrant, and they married in 1949. As way to serve her community, especially Black people and women, she ran for and won a position in the New York State Assembly in 1964. In 1968, Chisholm set her sights on an even higher office and began campaigning to join the US House of Representatives. That's when she started using her catchy slogan, "Unbought and Unbossed." She won in an upset victory over James Farmer, a well-known civil rights leader who used to be the head of the Congress of Racial Equality (CORE). She had become the first Black woman elected to Congress.

But she wasn't done. In January 1972, Chisholm announced yet another outrageous goal. Standing before a crowd of seven hundred people gathered at Concord Baptist Church, she launched a bid for the Democratic Party nomination for president of the United States. The audience cheered, but Chisholm immediately faced criticism. Because she was a Black woman, few people took her seriously as a candidate. They didn't understand why she should even try to run. But with the same boldness she had as a student, teacher, and Congress member, Chisholm pushed ahead. Her faith in God gave her courage. "I only look to God and my conscience for approval of what I am doing," she said.

Despite her faith, the odds of winning the nomination were never in her favor. She had much less money than the other candidates, so she couldn't afford much travel or advertisements or a large staff to help her. She did earn the approval of the Black Panther Party, who endorsed her, and she received enthusiastic support from poor and working-class people. But she faced opposition from leaders within the Democratic Party who did not think a woman should lead the country. White women also failed to give Chisholm much support. They saw her campaign as risky, and they did not share Chisholm's concerns with issues affecting the Black community. But it was the lack of support from Black men that stung Chisholm the most. They did not want to put their support or reputations behind a woman. Even though her bid for president was not successful, Chisholm still made history.

Chisholm stayed in politics and remained in Congress for almost ten more years, until 1981. She also was a founding member of the Congressional Black Caucus and the Democratic Women's Caucus. She stood against the Vietnam War, and she constantly pushed for more resources and better living conditions for people in the inner city. Underneath all her public service was a faith that influenced her actions. "America has the laws and the material resources it takes to ensure justice for all its people. What it lacks is the heart, the humanity, the Christian love that it would take." The spirit of justice gave Chisholm the courage to show people what the nation could be like if it really lived up to its promises.

MYRLIE EVERS-WILLIAMS

1933–

Myrlie Evers-Williams was born as Myrlie Beasley in Vicksburg, Mississippi,
on Saint Patrick's Day, March 17, 1933. In this segregated town, Myrlie
Beasley's world was Black, Christian, and mostly female. Three Black
women—her grandmother, great-great grandmother, and aunt—
taught Myrlie the value of education, hard work, and respect for self
and others. They also taught her the importance of faith in God.

Like many other Black people in that time, Myrlie grew up in a
Christian household. She remembers her mama singing gospel songs
such as "Pass Me Not, Oh Gentle Savior" while she was a child. For a
brief time in high school, Myrlie even experienced interracial worship
with white people, a very rare event in those days.

Myrlie met Medgar Evers during her first day on campus at Alcorn
A&M (now Alcorn State University). In 1950, Medgar was eight years
older than Myrlie, a junior at Alcorn, on the football team, and a
World War II veteran. Right away, Myrlie's grandmother and aunt
were protective. They did not want an older man and former soldier
who had lots of worldly experiences taking advantage of a sheltered
college freshman. But the couple's love was genuine and deep. "I had
prayed for months about Medgar and me, and by this time I was sure

we were right for each other," Myrlie remembers. They got married on Christmas Eve, 1951.

The couple relocated to Mound Bayou, Mississippi—an all-Black town founded in 1887—and began raising a family. Medgar got a job selling insurance, and his work took him to every part of the Mississippi Delta, the poorest region in the poorest state, and brought him face-to-face with the hardships of poor Black people like never before. This experience motivated him to get involved with the National Association for the Advancement of Colored People (NAACP).

Medgar became the first field secretary (regional leader) for the NAACP in Mississippi. The job brought him a lot of attention from people who didn't want things to change in the state, and the couple soon began receiving death threats, attacks on their home, and other forms of racial terrorism. When Medgar took the job, Myrlie recalled that she was "scared to death." But she understood the importance of the work. Myrlie Evers became a partner to Medgar in all his civil rights activities with the NAACP. They moved to Jackson, Mississippi, where she managed the administrative duties of the Mississippi office, and also offered Medgar advice and encouragement as they led voter registration drives, boycotts, and other demonstrations.

When a racial terrorist assassinated her husband in 1963 in front of their home, Myrlie Evers did not know how she could go on. She even thought of taking her own life. But she said, "For some reason—divine intervention I'm sure—I simply couldn't act on my intention." In the face of God and of her three children, Myrlie found a reason to keep living.

She moved the family to California for a new start. When she first got married, Myrlie had to quit school to take care of her home and family. But now she went back to college and got a degree to complete the educational journey she'd started at Alcorn. She then had several important jobs, including the national director for community affairs for a corporation and commissioner on the powerful Board of Public Works for the city of Los Angeles. She published her autobiography, *Watch Me*

Fly, and coedited *The Autobiography of Medgar Evers*. She started the Medgar and Myrlie Evers Institute in 1989. In 2013, fifty years after her husband's murder, she delivered the invocation at President Barack Obama's second inauguration. She was the first woman and the first layperson to do so. She was instrumental in seeing that the Jackson home where Medgar was shot was made into a national park and then into a national monument in 2023. She even fell in love with a man named Walter Williams and got married again.

Throughout her life, Evers-Williams remained active in the NAACP, the organization where Medgar had devoted the last of his energies. In the 1990s, when the NAACP had money troubles and people were losing confidence in it, she stepped up to help. She raised a lot of money for the organization and helped it get out of debt. She brought the NAACP back as a leader in the struggle for civil rights. And she became the face of the organization; her life and dedication represented its long struggle for progress. Her work at the NAACP served as more evidence of her faith in God and unbending will in the face of obstacles.

Her husband's murderer, Byron De La Beckwith, remained free for thirty years. Even though most people believed he had committed the crime, two all-white juries in separate cases refused to convict him. Myrlie Evers-Williams persisted in seeking justice. The case finally came to trial again in 1994. After the jury deliberated, Myrlie and her children assembled in the courtroom a few dozen feet from her husband's unremorseful killer. Finally, the verdict was read: "The jury finds the defendant, Byron De La Beckwith, guilty as charged." That moment came as a welcome and needed sign of the spirit of justice. It meant that with persistent effort and hope, accountability is possible.

As of this writing, Evers-Williams is still alive, and she lives by a notion that has carried her through many difficult days: "Though tragedy has shattered my world more than once, I have kept on keeping on. My faith in God and the strength of my forebears are like pillars holding up my soul, giving me an inner reserve of courage and hope to draw from."

SISTER THEA BOWMAN
1937–1990

Sister Thea Bowman was dying. The doctors had done their best to stop the cancer, but it had spread to many parts of her body. She could no longer walk and had to use a wheelchair, but she had been invited to speak at the United States Conference of Catholic Bishops, a big deal gathering of the most important leaders in the nation's Roman Catholic Church. She opened, as she often did, with a song. "Sometimes I feel like a motherless child ... A long way from home, a long, long way from home." She chose this song because, she explained, being Black and Catholic often felt "like being a second- or third-class citizen of the Holy City."

What Sister Bowman wanted to see was a diverse yet united community—the church as a "family of families." A church that would be a force for good in the world because of its unity. A church that would be able to "overcome the poverty—overcome the loneliness—overcome the alienation, and build together a Holy City, a new Jerusalem, a city set apart where they'll know that we are here because we love one another." Then she ended her speech as she began, with a song. She led this group of mostly white priests in an old song that had found new life in the civil rights movement, "We Shall Overcome."

Sister Thea Bowman has been called "the most well-known African

American religious sister in US Catholic history." Her fame partly comes from her dedication to racial reconciliation. Born as Bertha Bowman in Mississippi in 1937, she loved reading and music even as a toddler. She learned so quickly that she skipped first grade. Bowman was raised in a religious household and attended a Protestant Black church that taught her a simple and powerful faith. As a child, she was drawn to help others, and when Catholics began providing services for the poor in her hometown of Canton, she was eager to learn more about them. She was baptized into the Roman Catholic Church in 1947, when she was nine years old. Inspired by their daughter's enthusiasm, her parents joined the Catholic Church a few years later.

Bowman went to Holy Child Jesus Mission School in Canton. When she was a teenager, she sensed God was calling her to become a nun. It takes many years to go through all the education and spiritual guidance necessary to become a nun. So Bowman moved to Wisconsin to attend Viterbo College, a religious school run by the Sisters of Perpetual Adoration. Everything was new and different for Bowman. She was delighted to see snow for the first time, then shocked that winter lasted so long there. She went from an almost all-Black community to an almost all-white one. But she did well in school and completed her religious training. In 1956, she became Sister Thea Bowman, a nun with the Franciscan Sisters of Perpetual Adoration. When she graduated from college, she moved back to Mississippi to teach at the same Catholic school she had attended as a teenager. She also continued her education and earned a master's degree and eventually a PhD in English from the Catholic University of America.

After she'd been teaching for more than a decade, the Catholic bishop of Jackson, Mississippi, called Sister Bowman to be the Consultant for Intercultural Awareness for the diocese (region). In this role, she often worked with Black children and taught them songs, played games with them, and directed their plays. She tried to help them have a "better understanding of their own [African] heritage, the values and ways of thinking that made them who they are." She also traveled all over the

United States and to places like Nigeria, Kenya, and the Virgin Islands, always teaching about God's love for all people.

In 1983, Sister Bowman was diagnosed with breast cancer. But she still kept a packed speaking and traveling schedule. Toward the end of the talk she gave to the Catholic bishops, she cast a vision of the true Catholic Church. She explained that *Catholic* means "universal." The word speaks to the global nature of the Roman Catholic Church and the idea that everyone can be welcome in it. But Black Catholics experienced racism from their fellow white Catholics. Too often, the white priests and nuns segregated themselves from Black communities. They did not take the time to learn from or honor Black people. White Catholics usually kept Black Catholics out of leadership and decision-making. These behaviors led to racism, prejudice, and stereotypes.

Sister Bowman told these distinguished church leaders that a new era had dawned. Black Catholics were not going to be treated like children by white priests and leaders. Instead, they had a rich spirituality and a sense of community uplift that the church needed. "And now our Black-American bishops in the name of the Church universal have publicly declared that we as people of faith, as a Catholic people of God, have come of age, and it is time for us to be evangelizers of ourselves." Black people did not need to be rescued by white people; they only needed to be empowered.

The spirit of justice in Sister Thea Bowman led her to dedicate her life to serving others, teaching Black children in Mississippi, and working for racial unity in the Catholic Church. To those who knew Sister Bowman best, she spent her life well. Her friend, the renowned Black writer, educator, and poet Margaret Walker Alexander, expressed a sentiment many other held as well—"I think Sister Thea is a modern-day saint."

TONI MORRISON

1931–2019

Toni Morrison's Catholic faith taught her that God is love, and she wrote for the love of her people—Black people. Morrison, who died in 2019, was a world-famous writer. Some of her most famous books include the award-winning *Song of Solomon* and *Beloved*, which earned her the Pulitzer Prize for fiction writing. She also wrote a children's book called *Remember: The Journey to School Integration* and a book that's often read by young adults titled *The Bluest Eye*. Morrison's writing was fresh and new, and stood out in a book world that had been focused mainly on words by and about white people. Morrison explained that writing books was her way of supporting Black freedom and civil rights.

Morrison was born in 1931 in Lorain, Ohio, and her parents named her Chloe Wofford. At the age of twelve, she was baptized into the Catholic Church. It is common for people to take a new name when they come into the church through baptism, and she chose the name Anthony after St. Anthony of Padua. That's where she got the nickname Toni. Morrison always loved reading and did well in school. When it came time for college, she enrolled at Howard University, a historically Black school in Washington, D.C. Her hometown in Ohio had more racial integration than many places, so it was in the nation's capital that she first experienced the sting of segregation. For instance, she couldn't eat at certain restaurants or shop at certain stores. Morrison majored in English, and after graduating from Howard she went to Cornell University to earn a master's degree in English. She eventually taught at Howard and met her husband, Harold Morrison.

Morrison did not publish her first novel until she was thirty-nine years old. She and her husband had divorced by then, and she was raising two young sons on her own. She had to get up at four a.m. each morning to work on her book. Then she went to her job working as an editor at a publishing company. Eventually, her books did well enough that she could quit her job to become a full-time writer. She published her most famous book, *Beloved*, in 1987. It was inspired by the tragic and true story of an enslaved woman who escaped bondage and lost her child in the process. The heart-wrenching narrative of grief and regret insisted that people think about the evil of slavery, and people recognized Morrison as one of America's greatest writers.

As a Black woman in the US, Morrison had a deep understanding of how it felt to be constantly questioned and counted out. This experience gave her insights into the way racism works in the world. She called racism a distraction that "keeps you from doing your work." Morrison imagined words that created worlds where Black people were free. She did not use her books to explain what it was like to be Black to white people. She just wrote about regular life in a fascinating way and in the process told some of the best stories any writer in America had ever put on paper. She wrote as a woman and a Black person and simply let readers see life from her viewpoint.

Morrison wove faith and spirituality into her writing. In the stories she composed, there was always a sense of the supernatural, of a reality beyond what people could measure and define. Morrison knew that Black people were a spiritual people, because without faith in a higher power, anger over racism and inequality would have destroyed them from the inside out. She was inspired by Jesus, who was as innocent and weak as a lamb but who still had the power to rise back to life. Morrison did not have to write "religious" books. She simply created with the idea that religion—in many shapes and forms—was always present.

By writing for Black people, Toni Morrison opened up new possibilities for what stories deserved to be told and read. She helped Black people see themselves more clearly and offered readers of every race the gift of the Black experience. Morrison inspired all writers to be true to themselves and not worry about how people would judge them. She said, "If there's a book that you want to read, but it hasn't been written yet, then you must write it." Morrison showed the spirit of justice in her work by writing books for and about Black people so even the people who had often been left out and overlooked had a place in literature.

The **EARLY**
TWENTY-FIRST
CENTURY
2000–Today

Studying the history of racism and the struggle for justice can make us believe that these events are only about the past. The truth is the fight continues today. An important part of working for justice has always been gaining the right for all people to vote and passing laws that protect the most vulnerable people—and past generations were able to make many changes in those areas happen. But today, those rights they fought for are being threatened. Never fall into the trap of thinking that our civil rights cannot be rolled back and taken away. We have to always be working to protect and extend liberty. As professor and activist Angela Y. Davis said, "Freedom is a constant struggle."

January 6, 2021 was the worst attack on American democracy since the Civil War. Lawmakers were meeting in the US Capital building to officially certify the 2020 presidential election results. Joe Biden had won the election, but the former president, Donald Trump, spread a lie that he had won instead. In a speech that day, Trump encouraged his followers to march down to the Capitol. Thousands of people followed his call, and when they got there, they climbed walls, broke windows, invaded the building, shuffled through private papers, and did everything they could to forcefully stop the peaceful transfer of power from one president to the next. A man walked through the US Capitol building halls holding a large Confederate flag. The Confederates during the Civil War had not even gotten that far.

What happened on January 6 was part of the Make America Great Again (MAGA) movement. Many MAGA leaders want to roll back time to when certain people—especially rich, white men—controlled the country. Its leaders think that women shouldn't have the same rights as men and that they have too much independence, so they want to control women's votes and their bodies through new laws. They believe their president should have far more power than the Constitution allows. This takes power away from elected officials the American people chose through voting and lets the president do almost anything he wants even if most people oppose it.

Outside of the White House, the MAGA movement has also opposed racial justice. It calls almost any attempt to promote racial progress "woke." MAGA leaders have banned books that talk truthfully about racism in this country. They have opposed the Advanced Placement African American Studies course, a high school class meant to honor the history of Black people and prepare students for college. The MAGA movement has refused to give money to organizations that have Diversity, Equity, and Inclusion programs designed to promote racial understanding.

What's even worse is many people in the MAGA movement call themselves Christians. On January 6, 2021, a white supremacist group called the Proud Boys kneeled in prayer before storming the Capitol. The prayer leader asked God "to both represent you and represent our culture well. In Jesus's name we pray." And they all said amen, stood up, and broke into the Capitol.

Others that day used Christian symbols to represent the "holiness" of their mission. Outside the Capitol, they put up a huge wooden cross, and someone wearing black gloves with a printed image of finger bones on them clutched a Bible to his chest. People held signs reading, "Jesus is my Savior. Trump is my President."

These symbols were important because they showed that many of the people involved in storming the Capitol on January 6 were also part of a movement called white Christian nationalism (WCN). White Christian nationalism is a story people believe. It goes like this:

The United States was founded as a Christian nation on biblical principles and rose to become the richest, most powerful nation by following God's rules. But now the country is getting worse and worse because of "others," such as Muslims, Black people, LGBTQ+ people, women working outside the home instead of just being wives and mothers, and Black and brown immigrants coming into the United States. The only way to "save" America is by turning back to God and forcing the entire country to follow a strict set of Christian rules.

They are so set on making this vision a reality that they are willing to make voting harder, kick out government employees and politicians who don't do what they want, destroy the climate so oil companies keep getting richer, give tax breaks to billionaires while the poor and middle class suffer, and pack the Supreme Court with judges who agree with them and will issue rulings that extend their power. The situation is so dark that many people are saying that democracy as we know it or hoped it to be is coming to an end.

But a light pierces the darkness. There is a new justice generation rising to protect freedom once again. They are young people who have taken up the burden of justice because older generations have failed or refused. They are using the tools of technology and the digital age to make videos and social media posts designed to increase knowledge of what is going on and mobilize protest against it. They use phrases like "Black Lives Matter" to rally for racial justice. In 2020, they marched in historic numbers to protest police brutality after the murders of George Floyd, Breonna Taylor, and Ahmaud Arbery. The next justice generation may be new, but they are gaining strength from a historic source—the spirit of justice.

The Creatives

DANIELLE COKE BALFOUR, ANDRE HENRY, GARRISON HAYES, *and* COLE ARTHUR RILEY

Throughout US history, people have used their creative talents in the pursuit of justice. Elizabeth Keckley used dressmaking, Phillis Wheatley wrote poetry, and Toni Morrison published literature. That tradition continues today. Modern-day "creatives" use graphic arts, writing, social media, digital technology, and many other art forms not only to display beauty, but also to work for good in the world.

You can never predict when something will go viral, and it's not a plan for becoming rich or famous, but it does happen occasionally, and sometimes it happens for the right reasons. Danielle Coke Balfour began posting her original illustrations about Black History Month and historical figures such as Martin Luther King Jr. Then in the summer of 2020, her illustrations went viral. Her drawings said we needed justice and safety for Black people today, especially after a string of murders that year. Ahmaud Arbery, a Black man, was followed, shot, and killed by a group of white men because they thought he was trespassing in their mostly white neighborhood. Breonna Taylor was killed when police burst into her apartment in the middle of the night during a surprise raid that did not follow legal procedures. And George Floyd's murder ignited the nation when cell phone footage showed a white police officer kneeling on his neck for more than nine minutes, which led to Floyd's death. Coke Balfour gained more than 300,000 followers in one week! Since then, brands like Adobe, Toms, and Comcast have reached out to her for design work and advice. She even has her own collection at Target. Coke Balfour believes that art accesses the human heart in ways nothing else can. "Art invokes emotion, but activism encourages action, so when you put them both together, you're encouraging action by invoking emotion," she said.

Some people grow up with music in their house, and the tunes seep into their bones. They develop a love and appreciation for music at an early age and they just can't help singing, writing, or playing songs. That describes Andre Henry. His father was a reggae musician and filled his home with music and musicmaking. The content of his father's songs also sunk into Andre's heart. They were tunes about protest, justice, and defiance. So when Andre got older, he became a songwriter, musician, and singer. He describes his music as "anthems of resilience and revolution." Henry's racial justice awakening came in 2016, when a police officer shot and killed an unarmed Black man named Philando Castile near Minneapolis. Henry was studying theology at the time, and he knew God was outraged at racial injustice. So as a work of artistic activism, Henry dragged a one-hundred-pound boulder around in a cart. When curious people stopped him to ask what he was doing, he explained, "The boulder represents the burden that racism places on the Black psyche." He used a personal demonstration and his creativity as an artist to bring attention to an issue of racism. Henry continues to write songs of hope and inspiration, such as "We Are Tomorrow-Makers," "It Doesn't Have to Be This Way," and "How Long." Henry is a creative dedicated to shifting the culture with his art.

Some people just "get" how to make viral TikTok videos. They understand the popularity of short videos, they know how to edit and produce them for maximum interest, and, most importantly, they have smart things to say. Garrison Hayes is one of those people who is very good at using TikTok and social media in general. He has gained a TikTok following of 365,000 followers for his informative and entertaining videos about history and current events. Using a combination of savvy video editing and deeply researched content, several of his videos have gained over one million views. Some of his videos include "Will racism die off?" and "How Did Europeans Become White People?" Hayes served as a pastor and developed his skills as a creative while leading his church's digital strategy during the 2020 COVID-19 pandemic. In 2022, he was selected for the new Creator in Residence position at Mother Jones news organization. He blends history, race, and faith to inform an upcoming generation about the importance of the past and their responsibilities to work for justice in the present.

A lot of content on social media is fun or silly—and there's a place for that. There is also a place for deeper thoughts that remind us to take care of minds and hearts. That's where Cole Arthur Riley comes in. During 2020, she started the "Black Liturgies" project. Riley is a poet, and she wrote beautifully online about the value of Black life. She compared justice to breathing and shared how we need to "inhale" truth and beauty and "exhale" poisonous ideas and habits. Her deep thoughts brought her nearly half a million followers on Instagram, and led to her writing a couple books, including the New York Times bestseller This Here Flesh. Her work shows how justice is not just about what happens in the world, it's about what happens in our hearts as well.

A whole new squad of people who all have the spirit of justice inside them are rising up and using social media to spread the word. They are posting videos to teach people about history. Creating images and illustrations to say in pictures what words cannot communicate. Coming up with hashtags and trends that make their ideas zip across the world and fuel movements for justice. They are creatively using the spirit of justice to inspire and inform others online.

The Activists

LISA SHARON HARPER, LISA FIELDS, TERENCE LESTER, *and* LATASHA MORRISON

While there are many ways to fight for justice, activism is the most direct way of confronting racism—it is purposeful and designed to create positive change. The people in this section are activists for justice, whose faith and courage are making a difference.

Lisa Sharon Harper is the founder of FreedomRoad.us, an organization focused on helping people understand each other better and bringing unity between different groups of people. Harper is an activist. Wherever justice needs to show up, Harper does too. She's been to the border between the United States and Mexico to see how she can help immigrants. She has led and joined marches and protests in support of the idea that Black lives matter. She's traveled to different countries to learn from other people who are suffering and to discover how to help them. She leads groups of people on pilgrimages across the country, where they discuss issues such as slavery and freedom and faith and politics. These journeys are designed to share the stories of people often left out of the history books and to help people see justice issues from another perspective. Harper is also an author. Her book *The Very Good Gospel: How Everything Wrong Can Be Made Right* explained why the gospel of Jesus Christ is very good news. Harper writes about how Jesus came not just to give people a ticket to heaven, but to show his followers how to love and serve people now. Christians are supposed to bring peace and joy to the earth, just like Jesus did. That includes fighting against racism and working for all people to be free, Harper explains. Her activism is an expression of her beliefs about the gospel and her work is truly good news to people harmed by injustice.

Sometimes people are not sure if they believe in God, even if their family goes to church and prays before every meal. When everyone else seems positive that God is real, these people may feel like they need to hide their doubts. But Lisa Fields knows what it is like to have doubts about God. That is why she created the Jude 3 Project. In the Bible, Jude 3 is a verse that says, "Contend for the faith that was once for all entrusted to God's holy people." That means Christians should fight to make sure the truth the Bible shares is taught correctly. But it also means that doubt is a normal part of being a Christian and is nothing to be ashamed of—everyone has doubts sometimes. Fields helps people find and keep faith in God by creating short videos about topics such as "Why I Almost Left Christianity" and "Is Church a Safe Space?" that help explore their questions. She also wants Christians who disagree with each other to talk to each other so their differences can be worked out. Fields does this by hosting a conference every year called Courageous Conversations, where Christians who have different beliefs can discuss their disagreements and find out how they can understand each other better. She also made a film called Faith & Freedom about Juneteenth— the day on June 19, 1865, when enslaved people in Galveston, Texas, first learned about their freedom. It is the country's oldest celebration of Black freedom from slavery. Fields draws on the spirit of justice to help people find reasons to believe in God and live like Jesus.

Latasha Morrison is a bridge builder who wants to see people come together across the racial gap. That's why she started Be the Bridge in 2016. Morrison's passion for creating racial reconciliation through relationships partly came from being the only Black person working at a church in Austin, Texas. Her coworkers and others would often ask her questions and expect her to have all the answers about Black people and racial differences. After a while, she started a group that met once a month to talk about race and to understand each other better. Then, after she spoke at a huge conference in 2015, she started a Facebook group so people could connect there. It turned into Be the Bridge, which helps people start small groups and provides study guides to help them understand issues of race and unity better. Latasha got the attention of Facebook, and the social media business awarded her $100,000 to build her organization. Today, there are Be the Bridge groups all over the country and even the world. Morrison's work shows that you can have hard conversations and still speak gently and respectfully to the people you disagree with. She taps into the spirit of justice by being a peacemaker and bringing all kinds of people together.

Terence Lester knows from experience what it's like not to have a house. By the age of sixteen, he had dropped out of high school and joined a gang. Soon he was homeless, and at one point his situation became so overwhelming that he thought about taking his own life. When he was twenty years old, police arrested Lester. While he was in jail, someone shared the gospel of Jesus Christ with him, and it changed his life. Years later, Lester and his wife, Cecilia, started Love Beyond Walls to break down the barriers that keep people from understanding each other's experiences, raise awareness about those living with poverty and homelessness, and gather people to take action. His work involved national campaigns such as "Love Sinks In" that distributed portable sinks for people who didn't have homes to wash their hands and stay healthy during the COVID-19 pandemic. In 2016, he led the March Against Poverty, where he walked eight hundred miles from Atlanta to Washington, D.C., to bring attention to poverty in America. He also started the Dignity Museum, the first museum completely dedicated to the history of homelessness, which is run out of a repurposed shipping container. His family has also gotten involved. In 2024, he published a children's book with his daughter, Zion, called *Zion Learns to See*. It's a story based on real-life experiences where Zion "learns about people experiencing homelessness and [readers] see how she is moved to respond as she recognizes that all people matter to God." Lester's work is based on three ideas: 1) anyone can make a difference, 2) life is short, and 3) no one should feel invisible.

I even started my own organization called The Witness to help us move forward as a church and a nation in racial progress. Back in 2011, I noticed that many of the Christian churches and schools I attended did not have very many Black people. Pastors, professors, and other church members either did not talk about race much at all, or when they did they had very unhelpful, and sometimes even racist, ideas. The Witness came together as a way for Black Christians in majority white spaces to gain a sense of community and have a stronger voice as a group rather than as individuals. Today, The Witness uses a website, a yearly conference, and a podcast called Pass the Mic to talk about the Christian faith while highlighting the needs and concerns of Black people in particular.

Activism did not happen only during the racial justice movement; we still need activists today. While there are many ways to resist racism, activism is the most direct. One truth that aspiring activists today need to remember is that activism is a skill. No one is born knowing how to take effective action against injustice. It must be taught. People throughout this nation's history have understood that. During the civil rights movement, for example, marchers and protesters went through training. They learned about the need for nonviolence. How to cover up and protect their heads and bodies in case of a physical attack, and what to say and who to contact if they were ever arrested. Activists today also need training. It is not enough simply to be upset about an issue. Learn from people who came before you and see how they learned to protest and what worked and did not work. Then build on that action today.

Taking action for racial justice happens in all kinds of areas.

Unfortunately, every important part of life in the United States has been affected by racism. You can be an activist for racial justice by working in education. We still need more teachers from different racial and ethnic backgrounds so students can see someone who looks like them as an instructor who is sensitive to their needs. The legal system is often unfair if you are poor and Black. We need activists who will suggest new laws and policies and work hard to get them passed. Even the way pollution affects people is often determined by race. Areas that have more Black people or Latino people frequently have factories or chemical plants nearby that leak toxic waste and substances into the ground and water. These pollutants can cause many kinds of illnesses such as cancer, and we need people who will fight against big businesses that put money over people.

Activism also requires working together across all kinds of differences. One encouraging sign of progress today is that activists for racial justice include more people of all different kinds of races and ethnicities. During the George Floyd protests of 2020, for instance, Asian Americans, Native Americans, and Latinos marched and protested in support of Black lives. White people also joined demonstrations in large numbers. In some cases, there were even more white people at a protest than Black people. That would never have happened just a few decades ago. Now it is a sign of progress that people from different backgrounds recognize that their own freedom is wrapped up in the freedom of others. As another activist, Fannie Lou Hamer, said, "No one is free until everyone is free."

Each of the people in this section work in different areas—leading pilgrimages, helping people develop faith in God, working with houseless people, and building bridges of understanding. Yet they are all at the front of the struggle for racial justice today. As activists, they do hands-on work with people to improve their lives. They have become leaders who are empowered by the spirit of justice to guide people to higher levels of peace, trust, and understanding.

The Ministers

BRENDA SALTER MCNEIL, WILLIAM J. BARBER III, CLEMENTA PINCKNEY, *and* BERNICE KING

This section of the book has featured people with all kinds of jobs—musicians, social media content creators, nonprofit organization leaders. But one group of people has always been important in the journey of helping people understand faith and race—ministers. To minister means to serve. And church leaders and pastors serve as spiritual guides for people who want to grow in their relationship with God. They preach and teach from the Bible. They visit people when they are sick. They celebrate weddings and the birth of a new child. Ministers are also often the ones leading the way when it comes to challenging racism and showing people how to treat one another with dignity and respect.

Brenda Salter McNeil has been doing racial reconciliation and justice work for more than thirty years as a consultant, professor, and minister. She serves as an Associate Professor of Reconciliation Studies in the School of Theology at Seattle Pacific University. She is also an ordained pastor in the Evangelical Covenant Church (ECC). In her 2020 book, *Becoming Brave: Finding the Courage to Pursue Racial Justice Now*, she reflected on a nagging question she had about injustice: "What are you going to do about it?" She decided she must not only talk about racial reconciliation, she must *do* racial justice. "I decided to become brave—to say the things that I must say and to stand for the truth, regardless of the consequences." Drawing from her roots in the Black church tradition, she began speaking, teaching, and writing more forcefully about the need to work for racial justice from a place of love for God and love of neighbors. She teaches that all human beings are made in God's image, so they deserve to be treated carefully and respectfully. She demonstrates that differences are part of God's beautiful design, and the ways we are unlike each other do not need to divide us; instead, we celebrate them as another expression how God brings beauty into the world. Dr. Salter McNeil reminds everyone that the work of ministers and people of faith is not just to be nice each other but to change the systems, structures, and rules that make life harder for our neighbors.

William J. Barber III has been involved in racial justice since he was in kindergarten. His parents moved from Indianapolis, Indiana, to Washington County, North Carolina, to be part of a school desegregation initiative. They worked at the school and enrolled William in the kindergarten there. As a teenager, he became president of the NAACP youth council, and at the age of seventeen, he became student body president of an integrated high school. He also served as student government president in college. He continued his education and went on to earn a doctorate. He became the pastor of Greenleaf Christian Church in Goldsboro, North Carolina, in 1993 and has become a nationally known civil rights leader who combines faith and activism.

In 2013, he started Moral Mondays, a weekly gathering at North Carolina's state capital to protest discrimination and unjust policies. One voice can be small and unheard. A hundred voices all saying the same things are harder to ignore. That's why, in 2015, Barber started Repairers of the Breach. It is a movement that trains people in communities across the country how to come together so their cries for justice can be heard. And in 2018, he helped relaunch the Poor People's Campaign, the initiative Martin Luther King Jr. was building before he was assassinated. Rev. Barber has become a symbol of the next generation of justice leaders who base their work on the teachings of Jesus Christ.

When Clementa Pinckney was thirteen, he heard God's voice telling him, "I have called you to preach the gospel." Just a few months later, Pinckney presented himself as a ministry candidate in the African Methodist Episcopal (AME) denomination, which would allow him to start working toward becoming a minister. At eighteen years old, he was ordained to the ministry and became the pastor of a church. Even at this young age, he saw the link between believing in God and living that faith out in the real world. At twenty-three, he became the youngest person to be elected to the South Carolina state legislature. A few years later, he was elected state senator. The whole time, Pinckney was working as a pastor at several churches. Then, when he was thirty-six, he was made the pastor of the historic Emanuel AME church, also called Mother Emanuel, which played a major role in the fight for civil rights. He helped infuse youth into the elderly congregation but also built trust with longtime members. As a politician, Pinckney focused on serving his district, where most people were people of color and many lived below the poverty line. The way he combined preaching the word with holding an elected political office was a modern-day example of how the Black church and the Black community have been fighting and struggling for freedom for centuries. It was partly because of his work for justice that a young white man chose Rev. Pinckney's church for a deadly shooting. After sitting through the weekly Bible study meeting in the basement of Emanuel AME church, the young man started firing at the people who'd gathered there. When he finished, he had killed nine people. One of them was Clementa Pinckney. But Rev. Pinckney left an example of what it looks like to follow the spirit of justice . . . and of what it might cost to do so.

Bernice King is the youngest child of Martin Luther King Jr. and Coretta Scott King, and she continues the tradition of faith and activism that her parents taught her. Little Bernice was just five years old when her father was assassinated. But she grew up hearing about him and committed herself to studying his words and methods. She also had the powerful example of her mother, who raised the family while serving as an international human rights icon at the same time. At a young age, people told King that she sounded like her father. But her gift is about more than putting words together in a pleasing way. "I believe this is the real connection between me and my father—our words flow from a heart full of love, compassion, and conviction, out to the hearts of others." King has dedicated her life to continuing the nonviolent mission of both her parents. She attended the renowned Spelman College, became an ordained minister, and also earned her law degree and Master of Divinity degree. She currently serves as the CEO of the Martin Luther King Jr. Center for Nonviolent Social Change (also called the King Center). Places like the King Center exist because people aren't born knowing what works best to promote justice. It takes skills and training. The good news is anyone can learn what it takes to work for justice. King has developed the Nonviolence 365 training—"a love-centered way of thinking, speaking, acting, and engaging"—so that people can be leaders in the changes that lead to justice. She has received numerous awards and recognitions for her ongoing leadership in civil rights and is a living example of how the spirit of justice gets passed down from parents to children.

If religion is a force for good in the world, then religious leaders should be the first ones showing how this is possible. That's why ministers like the ones in this chapter are so important. They are living examples of how people of faith can be part of the solution that ends racism. People look to leaders to be models of what they believe about God and about justice. Ministers who have the spirit of justice shine like headlights on a car leading the way toward a better future.

CONCLUSION

The true stories of faith, race, and resistance in this book both teach and inspire. The people who came before us leave us lessons on liberation and what it means to do hard but necessary work. They have given us accounts—sometimes ordinary and sometimes epic—that show people facing unbelievable odds and obstacles with determination. We can honor these people by learning about their lives and seeing how we can continue their struggle for freedom today.

These stories span hundreds of years and are all very different. But there are certain qualities that make each individual stand out for their commitment to justice. They all embody faith, courage, imagination, and resilience. We can work to have these qualities in our lives too as we continue the tradition of the spirit of justice.

Faith

The Bible says, "For our struggle is not against flesh and blood, but against the rulers, against the authorities, against the powers of this dark world and against the spiritual forces of evil in the heavenly realms" (Ephesians 6:12). The women and men of faith who confronted racism in their day believed that racism was not just about the chains of slavery, the "Whites Only" signs of Jim Crow segregation, or the bars of prisons. They were facing off against forces you couldn't see, but which stood behind all kinds of injustices. Something that was not just wrong, it was evil. With the eyes of faith, they looked to Jesus to give them the power to resist racism and follow the Golden Rule to treat others the way they wanted to be treated.

The individuals we've met in *Stories of the Spirit of Justice* all had faith in God. Even though some white people tried to use the Bible as a tool for racism, Black people heard the message of freedom in the words of Jesus Christ. In the Bible, the book of Exodus talks about how the Egyptians enslaved the Hebrew people. Black people under slavery in the US saw a reflection of their own experience in these stories. They understood what it was like to be victims of injustice and still continue to work for their liberty. Of course, you don't have to be Christian or practice religion to be against injustice. But the story of resistance to racism would not be complete without acknowledging the faith in God so many in the movement shared.

Courage

When it comes to fighting racism, we don't have a how-to problem, we have a want-to problem. In other words, racism continues today not because we don't have ideas about how to fight it. Give almost anyone a paper, a pen, and five minutes, and they will come up with suggestions for how we can push back against racism. The real problem with racism is that not enough people *want* to fight it. That is why in the hundreds of talks I have given to crowds of people all over the country, I constantly emphasize courage. Courage is not the absence of fear but the resolve to do what is right in the face of it.

Courage can grow. The more you exercise it, the more of it you have. The people in this book all demonstrated courage. Many of them faced rejection, physical violence, and emotional pain for standing up for righteousness. People like Martin Luther King Jr. and Medgar Evers were killed for their commitment to justice. Even those who survived the struggle did so at great cost to themselves, their families, and their friends. But through the spirit of justice, they found the courage to confront their fears and move forward.

Imagination

When Martin Luther King Jr. said, "I have a dream," he was also saying, "I have imagination." Justice requires imagination—the ability to see a future and possibilities that do not yet exist.

Think about the imagination it took for Robert Smalls to come up with a plan to steal a Confederate slave ship. He had to envision every phase of the risky plan—the time when the white sailors would leave, which of his fellow enslaved people would accompany him, the signals necessary to sail past enemy ships, and a backup plan in case something went wrong. Harriet Tubman had to imagine all kinds of ways to disguise herself and avoid slave catchers on her many trips back to the South to free others. Charles Hamilton Houston had to imagine a legal strategy to challenge the laws that made racial segregation legal. People who fought against racism had to imagine a world of equality that had never existed before. The spirit of justice brings us to the mountaintop and lets us see a promised land beyond the valley of injustice.

Resilience

In every era of history, the people who make the most progress resisting racism are the people who simply won't quit. At some level, every positive example in history is a story of resilience. It is a story about people facing many challenges and obstacles who kept pushing ahead.

No matter how scary the forces against you are, they cannot win when you refuse to give up. That is resilience.

We all would have understood if Coretta Scott King chose to live a quiet life after her husband's murder. But she kept pursuing the causes of civil rights and human rights. The spirit of justice inside her stirred a desire to make sure what happened to her family would not happen to others. As a result, she became a living example of how to fight for racial justice, and she motivated others to follow her path.

From one perspective, the fact that we still need to resist racism after hundreds of years is sad. It means that injustice is still harming people today. From another perspective, though, we can take heart that the strength in us is greater than the powers of hatred against us. Nothing can stop a people who refuse to stop.

The Spirit of Justice Speaks

Myrlie Evers-Williams went through pain and loss that no one should have to bear. With the crack of a gun, she became a widow and a single parent. In the face of this devastating theft of life, she continued her work for justice. Evers-Williams managed the NAACP's first state office in Mississippi, a public job that left her open to constant threats and intimidation. She persevered for thirty years while her husband's killer walked free until a jury finally convicted him in 1994. She went back to school and earned her bachelor's degree, wrote books, remarried, raised a family, and became national chair of the board for the NAACP, leading the organization her husband once worked for.

Even though people like Myrlie Evers-Williams worked their entire lives for progress, there is still work to be done. There are attacks against learning the true history of race in the United States. People are shutting down programs designed to help Black people and other people of color in schools and businesses. Racist groups and organizations are publicly protesting against racial progress. The struggle for justice never ends.

But there is good news. The same spirit of justice that empowered generations in the past is available to you today. It has been there for people across time whenever they needed it. It is here when you need it too. And, sadly, it is always needed. So pause for a moment. Breathe. Listen closely enough and you will hear a still, small voice encouraging you to declare your dignity and stand up for righteousness.

The spirit of justice still speaks.

BIBLIOGRAPHY

THE COLONIAL ERA

Mark Charles and Soong-Chan Rah. *Unsettling Truths: The Ongoing, Dehumanizing Legacy of the Doctrine of Discovery*. InterVarsity Press, 2019.

Olaudah Equiano. *The Interesting Narrative of the Life of Olaudah Equiano, or Gustavus Vassa, the African*. Public domain, 1789.

THE REVOLUTIONARY ERA

US Declaration of Independence. Public domain, 1776.

Phillis Wheatley. *Poems on Various Subjects, Religious and Moral*. Public domain, 1773.

"Prince Hall: Bound for Greatness." Medford Historical Society and Museum, https://www.medfordhistorical.org/medford-history/africa-to-medford /prince-hall/.

Prince Hall. "Petition to the Massachusetts Legislature." Public domain, 1777.

DuSable Museum, Chicago, IL.

THE ABOLITIONIST MOVEMENT

David W. Blight. *Frederick Douglass: Prophet of Freedom*. Simon & Schuster, 2018.

Philippe R. Girard. *The Memoir of General Toussaint Louverture.* Oxford University Press, NY, 2014.

David Walker. "David Walker's Appeal, in Four Articles, Together with a Preamble, to the Coloured Citizens of the World, but in Particular, and Very Expressly, to Those of the United States of America." Presented 1829, rev. 1830; reprinted by Affordable Classics Limited, 2021.

Rosetta Douglass Sprague. "Anna Murray Douglass: My Mother as I Recall Her." Delivered before the Anna Murray Douglass Union, WCTU, May 10, 1900, Washington, D.C.

"Paul Cuffe, a Brief Biography." Paul Cuffe: An African American and Native American Heritage Trail website, https://paulcuffe.org/biography/.

THE CIVIL WAR AND RECONSTRUCTION

Cate Lineberry. *Be Free or Die: The Amazing Story of Robert Smalls' Escape from Slavery to Union Hero.* St. Martin's, 2017.

Sarah Pruitt. "5 Things You May Not Know About Abraham Lincoln, Slavery and Emancipation." History.com. September 21, 2012. https://www.history.com/news/5-things-you-may-not-know-about-lincoln-slavery-and-emancipation.

National Holiday Proclamation signed by President Joe Biden, 2021.

Kate Clifford Larson. *Bound for the Promised Land: Harriet Tubman, Portrait of an American Hero.* One World Ballantine, 2004.

Elizabeth Keckley. *Behind the Scenes, or Thirty Years a Slave, and Four Years in the White House.* Public domain, 1868; reprinted by Eno, 2016.

THE JIM CROW ERA

Eric Foner. *A Short History of Reconstruction.* Perennial Library, 1990.

Robert Whitaker. *On the Laps of Gods: The Red Summer of 1919 and the Struggle for Justice That Remade a Nation.* Crown, 2008.

Paula J. Giddings. *Ida, a Sword Among Lions: Ida B. Wells and the Campaign Against Lynching.* Amistad, 2008.

Estrelda Y. Alexander. *Black Fire: 100 Years of African American Pentecostalism.*

InterVarsity Press, 2011.

Anna Julia Cooper. *A Voice from the South*. Aldine, OH, 1892; reprinted by Amazon Classics, 2016.

Genna Rae McNeil. *Groundwork: Charles Hamilton Houston and the Struggle for Civil Rights*. University of Pennsylvania Press, 1983.

THE CIVIL RIGHTS ERA

Jerry Mitchell. *Race Against Time: A Reporter Reopens the Unsolved Murder Cases of the Civil Rights Era*. Simon & Schuster, 2020.

Barbara Ransby. *Ella Baker and the Black Freedom Movement: A Radical Democratic Vision*. University of North Carolina Press, 2003.

Keisha Blaine. *Until I Am Free: Fannie Lou Hamer's Enduring Message to America*. Beacon Press, 2021.

Martin Luther King Jr. *Where Do We Go from Here: Chaos or Community?* Beacon Press, 1967; reprinted 2010.

Coretta Scott King and Barbara Reynolds. *Coretta: My Life, My Love, My Legacy*. Henry Holt, 2017.

Dorothy Height. *Open Wide the Freedom Gates: A Memoir*. Public Affairs, 2003.

THE LATE TWENTIETH CENTURY

Aram Goudsouzian. *Down to the Crossroads: Civil Rights, Black Power, and the Meredith March Against Fear*. Farrar, Straus, and Giroux, 2014.

Jemar Tisby. *The Color of Compromise: The Truth about the American Church's Complicity in Racism*. Zondervan Reflective, 2019.

James H. Cone. *The Cross and the Lynching Tree*. Orbis, 2011.

Shirley. Biopic directed by John Ridley; produced by Royal Ties Production; distributed by Netflix. 2024.

Chisholm '72: Unbought and Unbossed. Documentary directed by Shola Lynch; produced by Phil Bertelsen and Shola Lynch/Realside Productions. Originally aired on PBS stations February 7, 2005.

Myrlie Evers and Melinda Blau. *Watch Me Fly: What I Learned on the Way to Becoming the Woman I Was Meant to Be*. Little, Brown, 1999.

BIBLIOGRAPHY

Charlene Smith and John Feister. *Thea's Song: The Life of Thea Bowman.* Orbis, 2009.

Toni Morrison. *Remember the Journey to School Integration.* Clarion Books, 2004.

Toni Morrison. *The Bluest Eye.* Holt, Rinehart, and Winston, 1970; reprinted by Vintage, 2007.

THE EARLY TWENTY-FIRST CENTURY

Philip S. Gorski and Samuel L. Perry. *The Flag and the Cross: White Christian Nationalism and the Threat to American Democracy.* Oxford University Press, NY, 2022.

Andre Henry. *All the White Friends I Couldn't Keep: Hope—and Hard Pills to Swallow—About Fighting for Black Lives.* Convergent Books, 2022.

Cole Arthur Riley. *This Here Flesh: Spirituality, Liberation, and the Stories That Make Us.* Convergent Books, 2023.

Lisa Sharon Harper. *The Very Good Gospel: How Everything Wrong Can Be Made Right.* Waterbrook, 2016.

Latasha Morrison. *Be the Bridge: Pursuing God's Heart for Reconciliation.* Waterbrook, 2019.

Terence and Zion Lester. *Zion Learns to See: Opening Our Eyes to Homelessness.* IVP Kids, 2024.

Brenda Salter McNeil. *Becoming Brave: Finding the Courage to Pursue Racial Justice Now.* Brazos Press, 2021.

Nonviolence 365® Training program by the King Center. Accessible via https://thekingcenter.org/nonviolence365-training/.

I Am the Spirit of Justice

Jemar Tisby with Malcolm Newsome

Illustrated by Nadia Fisher

In the picture book *I Am the Spirit of Justice*, Jemar Tisby demonstrates that that arc of history bends toward equality. Throughout, the spirit of justice is personified as it moves through time, loving the oppressed and supporting the freedom fighters throughout America's history. The poetic text not only informs readers of the countless and often nameless people who have taken up the fight, it also inspires them to continue working for equality for all.

I Am the Spirit of Justice is a companion to Jemar Tisby's *The Spirit of Justice* for kids four and up. This beautiful and sweeping book is a great introduction to the history of civil rights for the youngest readers and an important addition to the libraries of anyone working for justice.

I Am the Spirit of Justice is ideal for:

- introducing children to important figures in the history of the civil rights movement
- inspiring young readers to see the importance of justice in our world
- teachers and librarians looking for resources for civil rights education, with an included bibliography and suggestions for further reading

AVAILABLE WHEREVER BOOKS ARE SOLD!

The Spirit of Justice
Jemar Tisby

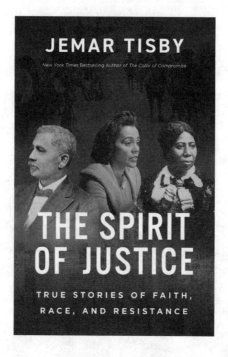

The Spirit of Justice reveals the stories of the people who fought against racism and agitated for justice—and what we can learn from their example, their suffering, their methods, and their hope.

How is it that people still work for change after continuously seeing the worst of humanity and experiencing the most demoralizing setbacks? What keeps them going? It is that spirit of justice that rises up "like a war horse," as Myrlie Evers-Williams famously said. It is a sense in the hearts of people who hunger and thirst for righteousness.

In this book, award-winning author Jemar Tisby will open your eyes to the "pattern of endurance" in the centuries-long struggle for Black freedom in America. Through a historical survey of the nation from its founding to the present day, this book gives real-world examples of people who opposed racism, how they did it, what it cost, and what they gained for themselves and others.

For those who were galvanized by Tisby's call to action in his acclaimed *The Color of Compromise*, this book will inspire you to see past the complicity of the church and gain the determination to join the fight for racial justice, no matter the cost.

As Tisby writes, "The Spirit of justice is always at work to inspire followers of Christ to undertake acts of liberation and bear witness to the good news of their savior."

AVAILABLE WHEREVER BOOKS ARE SOLD!

How to Fight Racism Young Reader's Edition

Jemar Tisby with Josh Mosey

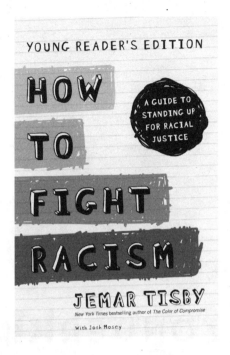

Racism is pervasive in today's world, and in the wake of protests and a call for change, many kids are eager to confront it but aren't always sure how. Jemar Tisby, author of *How to Fight Racism* and *The Color of Compromise*, believes we need to move beyond mere discussions about racism and begin equipping young people with the practical tools to fight against it.

In *How to Fight Racism Young Reader's Edition*, Dr. Tisby uses history to explore how racism has affected America since before its founding and how it's continued to grow, as well as examines how true social justice is rooted in the Christian faith. In a format that provides kids with a handbook for pursuing racial justice, readers ages 8-12 will discover:

- hands-on suggestions and real-world examples of change they can put into action
- practical ideas for confronting racism and social injustice in their everyday lives, and how they can use Christian values to change the narrative around race
- the ARC of racial justice—Awareness, Connection, and Relationships—that help form an anti-racist mindset
- ways to evaluate their actions and promote biblical principles

AVAILABLE WHEREVER BOOKS ARE SOLD!